THE CHINESE DI

"Courageous and thought-provoking, an honest and articulate appraisal of the Malaysian situation today."
Lee Su Kim, Associate Professor of English, Universiti Kebangsaan Malaysia, Malaysia

"Now comes a book that will be just as controversial [as Mahathir Mohamad's *The Malay Dilemma*]—*The Chinese Dilemma*." **The Edge**

"Ye Lin-Sheng's *The Chinese Dilemma* is a critique of Malaysia's New Economic Policy (NEP), rigorously implemented since the political ascendancy of Mahathir Mohamad in the 1970s. The NEP has been the subject of much international criticism for unambiguously promoting preferential treatment of the indigenous Malays above their Chinese and Indian counterparts in the population. However, Ye argues that this may very well have been the price required for turning Malaysia into the multicultural success that it is. The successful application of affirmative action as a means to resolving race conflict in Malaysia is compared to the failed affirmative-action programmes for the blacks in the U.S. He finds himself pondering on the irony that while Western nations enshrine equality and democracy in their constitutions they are not able to deliver equality and democracy to certain races in their populations."
Mabel Lee, University of Sydney, Australia

"This is a highly controversial book and, had it been released at the same time as Mahathir's *The Malay Dilemma*, it would probably have been banned too. What the author has done is to discuss publicly issues which are often discussed privately, but because he has adopted an entirely non-partisan view, he will probably earn very little support. Those who can read the book rationally rather than emotionally still form a small segment of Malaysia's population. For someone trained in the physical sciences, the author has been able to put forward his views with great precision. This book should be read by the younger generation of Malaysians. It may help the unprejudiced mind to see things in a better perspective."
Khoo Kay Kim, Professor of Malaysian History, University of Malaya, Malaysia

THE CHINESE DILEMMA

"This important and convincing study points to the inherent good sense and high social benefit of what is often ignorantly disparaged—Malaysia's racially biased constitutional system. The author, a Chinese Malaysian, lucidly expounds the logic and describes the success of Mahathir's policy of tilting the playing field so as to help the Malays establish and maintain themselves as confident social players against the Chinese minority, who without that handicap would have continued to dominate the economy—and thus inevitably become target for the violently expressed resentment of the relegated majority. The Malaysian example, as demonstrated here, shows that, given rational and far-sighted governance, positive discrimination can lead to social harmony through shared prosperity."

Neville Maxwell, Visiting Fellow, Contemporary China Centre, Australian National University, Canberra, Australia

"This is perhaps the most controversial, contentious and yet challenging analysis argued within the theoretical framework of the 'Malay Dilemma'. To the best of my knowledge, there has never been anything like this submitted by a Malaysian and particularly, if I might say so, a rare case of a Malaysian Chinese."

Collin Abraham, former Associate Professor of Sociology, Universiti Sains Malaysia, Malaysia

"*The Chinese Dilemma* is a timely reminder of the central issues in Malaysian politics. The author displays an intimate knowledge of racial politics in Malaysia and around the world. Arguments like this one will ensure much-needed debate about the choices facing Malaysia's Chinese community."

Peter van Onselen, Department of International Relations, University of New South Wales, Sydney, Australia

"[*The Chinese Dilemma*] offers interesting reflections on how Australia has looked from Malaysia. This latest book is an invaluable new interpretation of a period and place in recent regional history of major importance to Australia—for business, government, and the informed media. No one in Australia should deal in or with Malaysia without a knowledge of the issues it raises."

Duncan Campbell, former Australian Deputy High Commissioner to Malaysia (1968-1971)

The Chinese Dilemma

YE LIN-SHENG

East West Publishing Pty Ltd
Australia

Published by
East West Publishing Pty Ltd
P.O. Box 857
Kingsford
New South Wales 2032
Australia

E-mail: *info@eastwestpublishers.com.au*
Website: *www.eastwestpublishers.com.au*

1st edition
1st printing ... February 2004
2nd printing ... April 2004
3rd printing ... August 2004
4th printing ... April 2005
5th printing ... May 2008

The National Library of Australia Cataloguing-in-Publication entry

Ye, Lin-Sheng, 1933-
The Chinese dilemma.

Bibliography.
Includes index.
ISBN 0 9751646 0 0
ISBN 0 9751646 1 9 (pbk)

1. Chinese – Malaysia – Economic conditions. 2. Chinese – Foreign countries. 3. Malaysia – Economic conditions. 4. Malaysia – Economic policy. I. Title.

338.9595

for my family and friends
across the racial spectrum

ABOUT EAST WEST PUBLISHING

East West Publishing is a new publisher dedicated to exploring the politics, economics, culture and history of the nations of Asia. Although it is home to two-thirds of the world's population, this vast, diverse mass of people has spent the modern era overshadowed by Europe and America. Now, at the dawn of the 21st century, the balance of power and influence is beginning to change. Our aim is to foster the appreciation of different national and ethnic values—to bridge the gulf of misunderstanding that exists between those contrasting world-views we call East and West.

CONTENTS

PREFACE

I HAVE DWELT on "the Chinese dilemma" in Malaysia ever since I read Mahathir Mohamad's *The Malay Dilemma* (1970) more than a quarter of a century ago. In 1990 I began to put my thoughts down on paper. My progress was tortuous as I lacked the necessary erudition and found it difficult to gather material.

In 1992, I came across Lynn Pan's *Sons of the Yellow Emperor: The Story of the Overseas Chinese* (1990). Two thoughts struck me as I read this saga about the millions of Chinese who left the shores of China to seek their fortunes overseas. The first was that the persecution, cruelty and humiliation these Chinese suffered were perpetrated not by the indigenous peoples of the lands to which they had journeyed, but by the white colonisers—the Spaniards in Manila, the Dutch in Batavia, the British in Australia and Canada, and the white Americans in California.

My second thought was that if I could enlist Lynn Pan's assistance I might be able to tell my story and tell it better. I thought that if I could tap into her command of the English language and her familiarity with the history of the Chinese diaspora, my attempts to spell out the Chinese dilemma might get somewhere.

I got in touch with her through her publisher and we met half a dozen times to talk at length about the issues set out in this book. Among other things, she introduced me to Gunnar Myrdal's *An American Dilemma: The Negro Problem and Modern Democracy* (1940) and Thomas Sowell's *Preferential Policies: An International Perspective* (1990). Reading these books, I became more convinced than ever that the Chinese dilemma in Malaysia called for someone to articulate it.

I am most grateful to her for agreeing to act as scribe. I now know that without her I would have continued to flounder for many more years without result! I must also record my thanks to my Girl Friday Xu Bingyuan, who for so long has typed and retyped many a simple sentence; and to my classmate Chen Hanqiang, whose thoughtful insights and knowledge of the Malaysian Chinese community have informed my understanding of many issues.

I am responsible for the general thrust of the book, the views expressed in it and for any awkwardness in the way I argue my case. Discussing these views with friends and showing them an earlier draft of the manuscript in the closing stages of the book was a salutary exercise. While conscious of the emotions evoked by the subject matter, I must confess to my surprise at finding how sensitive it has remained. I can only ask my many friends across the racial spectrum to believe me, or at any rate to give me the benefit of the doubt, when I say that the arguments I put forward are not intended to score points for any side, but rather to foster understanding between the peoples of our country.

Ye Lin-Sheng
Kuala Lumpur
June 2003

CHAPTER 1

INTRODUCTION

THE TITLE of this book echoes Dr. Mahathir Mohamad's *The Malay Dilemma*. This is entirely deliberate. Almost all Malaysians will now have heard of *The Malay Dilemma*, and though I am probably right in thinking that most will not have actually read it, few will be unfamiliar with its main thrust.

I first read the book in Singapore in 1970, shortly after it was published. The book had promptly been banned as being too inflammatory by the government of Tunku Abdul Rahman, the nation's father figure and first prime minister. Its appearance had alarmed the non-Malay half of the country's multiracial population, which had collectively deemed its contents as racist or, in local parlance, "ultra." Abroad, foreign observers pronounced it unscientific, racist and shocking. It was certainly candid and even blunt, I myself thought, and some of its strictures on the Chinese did sound misdirected to me, but whether it was racist, I was not so sure.

All the same, you could sense some unease in even the publisher, whose own note at the front of the book clearly anticipates misgivings in some quarters. I quote: "Not all historians will agree with Mahathir's interpretation of events, historic and recent, in Malaysia and Singapore. This is certain to be a controversial book, and assuredly the author will be called upon to defend many of his statements and claims, indeed even perhaps the accuracy of his historical and biological data. This is not an objective work." And, as if an explanation were called for, the publisher tells the reader that the book is nevertheless published because "this is what an educated, modern, progressive Malay thinks and believes. These are his reactions to the problems of the day, the pressing problems that beset Malaysia. This is how a politically-inclined Malay understands the past, explains the behaviour of his own people and the behaviour of immigrants, and foresees the future ..."

It is hard to read these words without a sense of irony, because we now know what readers could not have known then, that what the author saw for the future, considered so extremist then, would become the future. What had seemed so contentious then would become government policy, a fact of everyday living. The publisher had meant us to read the book as a guide to the thinking of a modern-minded Malay, but it was actually much more than that, more even than a clue to the mind of a would-be prime minister. It was in fact a blueprint for the next twenty-odd years. Its ideas for the betterment of the Malays would find concrete form in the New Economic Policy (NEP), launched in 1971 to increase Malay economic power and breed a Malay bourgeoisie.

The book deals with the relations between the two main races in Malaysia: the indigenous Malays, who form roughly half the population; and the immigrant Chinese, who make up a third. I call them "races" rather than the more fashionable "ethnic groups" because, as a businessman rather than a scholar, I simply find the word "race" clearer. I am told that you are supposed to eschew words like "race" and "racial" these days (partly because of the unhappy uses of these terms around the time of World War II), but as this is not a learned treatise, I hope I may be forgiven for my violation of such taboos.

Stated simply, Mahathir's proposition is that the Malays are ill-equipped by their racial traits, upbringing and conditioning to compete against the commercially advanced and acquisitive Chinese in their midst. The Chinese dominated the domestic sector of the economy (that is, the part not owned by British interests), all the more so since the Malay achievement of independent nationhood, confirming the Malay in his fear that he had regained his country from the colonial British only to have it taken from him by the Chinese.

This was an untenable situation, one that could spark off a repeat of the May 1969 crisis. May 13, 1969 was a turning point in Malaysian history, the date on which communal tensions flared up in rioting. "What went wrong?" asks Mahathir in his book. Why this violent rift between the Malays and the Chinese? His answer is that there can be no racial harmony so long as the imbalance of economic power remains. And that imbalance can only be redressed by giving Malays preferential treatment over the other races.

Push the scales to their advantage, Mahathir argues. Give them a better shot at business, for so long considered the special preserve of the Chinese. Left alone, the Chinese may well deliver Malaysia faster to the common goal of national prosperity. But should the Malay stand aside and, poor but proud, watch his country prosper under the Chinese? Or should he demand a share in that prosperity, even at the cost of slowing down the economy? This, Mahathir says, is the Malay dilemma. It is one which Malays are reluctant to bring out into the open, inhibited as they are by the value their social code attaches to courtesy, accommodation and self-restraint.

As a result, they are faced with the prospect of becoming dispossessed in their own country. Mahathir draws an analogy: "The Malays and the Red Indians of America are more or less in the same category. Malays are accepted as the indigenous people of the country, but the country is no longer exclusively theirs."

This has come of the mass immigration of Chinese (and to a lesser extent Indians) during the British colonial period. It is not possible to describe the Malay dilemma and not discuss the British, any more than it is possible to write about the Malay dilemma and not talk of the Chinese. In his book Mahathir does deal with the British and the Chinese, but of course only as aspects of the Malay problem. The British part in this problem has had its detractors as well as its apologists. But we have yet to see a Chinese follow-up to *The Malay Dilemma*.

In those days, whenever the subject of Mahathir's book cropped up in conversation, people would invariably ask, "Is he anti-Chinese?" After all, in his book he seems displeased with what he sees as Chinese insensitivity to the Malay plight. However, I myself thought that it must have been a most painful book for Mahathir to have to write, because to argue in favour of protecting the Malays against the challenge of the Chinese, he had first to acknowledge the inadequacies of his race. He had to suggest that it is the Malays' handicap, their inferior position, which earns them the advantage he wants to see conferred on them.

To pull the Malay up, it is generally believed, is to push the Chinese down. This is a belief that is tenaciously held both at home and abroad, but how much truth is there to it? Who are the Chinese who feel most aggrieved? Mahathir calls for a change in certain Malay habits and attitudes; what are the changes required of the Chinese? Over the years, I had toyed with the idea of writing a book examining just such questions. I thought of calling it *The Chinese Dilemma*, riding, obviously, on the coat-tails of Mahathir's notoriety. I thought that such a book might explore, just as Mahathir's has done for the Malays, those traits of culture and character which bear on the Chinese situation in Malaysia. But as to what else it would deal with, I must admit I was none too clear. Indeed I would be hard put to spell out what the Chinese dilemma is.

To be in a dilemma, I see from the dictionary, is to be faced with a choice between equally unwelcome possibilities. So what are the unfavourable alternatives facing the Chinese in Malaysia, or the Malays for that matter? I look to Mahathir's book for a lead, and I find that there isn't always an either/or sense to his use of the word. He does point to one set of alternatives facing the Malays: the choice between speaking up and admitting their shortcomings, and remaining silent and staying poor. But in his other usages the word "dilemma" is often interchangeable with "predicament" or "difficult situation." Perhaps this is why people who try to summarise his book find it so hard to spell out exactly what the horns of the Malay dilemma are. I decide to make life easier for myself by adopting the looser usage too.

One reason I did not until now put pen to paper, I suppose, was that as a businessman I wasn't convinced that I was the right person to tackle such a book. For a time it had also seemed to me that the need for such a book had passed. Surely everything that can be said about Chinese-Malay relations has been said already? Can anything new be added? *The Malay Dilemma* was published in the immediate aftermath of the May 1969 race riots. Today, those riots are a distant memory. And since Malaysia has not been riven by racial and religious conflicts of the kind that has ravaged the former Yugoslavia and elsewhere—and good news doesn't sell—a book on race would serve no useful purpose.

Or so I thought. But I was mistaken. Whenever I see racial violence break out in various parts of the world on my television screen, I think that other Chinese must now feel as I do, thankful to be a citizen of Malaysia, and allow that it is a good country to live in and that its government has run it wisely and skilfully. But what has given me food for thought has been the discovery that many Chinese still do not share my feelings, and a question I find myself constantly asking is: "Why not?" It is that question, I suppose, which prompted me to revive the idea of the book.

In a way I am glad that so many years have passed since I first conceived the idea, because in the lapse of time some of my views have changed and also events and developments both at home and in the world at large have helped put the issue of race in Malaysia in clearer perspective. I did finally put pen to paper, completing the book in 1994. But a feeling that my conclusions were too pat and that the prosperity we were enjoying at the time made it too easy for me to argue my case, held me back from rushing into print. Would tougher times make a nonsense of my convictions? In hindsight I'm glad I hesitated. We have since been sorely tested, by an Asia-wide financial crisis no less than by domestic discord, but these changes have if anything confirmed me in my convictions, and my views have remained intact.

As for what my views are, I am told by some of my friends that they are unconventional for a Chinese. I write as someone who is proud of his Chinese origin. But I am also trying to write as a fair-minded citizen; and as a fair-minded citizen, I feel I should challenge the conventional Chinese perception of their position in Malaysia. I should add here that my references to "Malaysia" should be understood to relate throughout to peninsular, or West Malaysia—Sabah and to a lesser extent Sarawak having a somewhat different racial complexion which it is beyond the scope of this book to consider.

I should explain that my views are those of a seventy-year-old, one whose working life began in the colonial period. I was born to parents who migrated to Malaya from China in 1931. Rare for Chinese migrants of the time, they were well educated—my mother had had a high school education and had been a teacher, while my father was a Political Science graduate of the renowned American missionary university, St. John's, in Shanghai.

My upbringing could have been typically immigrant Chinese; that is to say, I could have gone, like some of my siblings, to a Chinese-language school where the medium of instruction was Mandarin and the curriculum calculated to imbue the pupils with a Chinese world view and a sense of Chinese history. In other words, I could have been a Chinese-educated Malaysian. But I am not. Instead, I would describe my upbringing as being typically Malaysian English-speaking and urban. I started in Chinese school before the Japanese Occupation, but then switched almost immediately to the English-medium Christian Brothers English School. Over the years my mother did her best to cajole me into attending Chinese classes—so that, as she put it, "You won't turn out a bull" (meaning "rough and boorish") like the white man. But I can't say she had much success, and I was like many another urban Malayan Chinese in my orientation towards English.

For more than ten years, apart from a sprinkling of Indians and Eurasians, my classmates were entirely Chinese. It was not until my last year at school, in 1951, that I had a Malay for a classmate, my first and only, as it happened. Later, studying Engineering in Kuala Lumpur, I had a little more contact with Malays; and a lot more when, as a government employee, I had them as colleagues, subordinates and superiors, and particularly when I worked in the rural areas. Were I Chinese-educated throughout my school years, I would have gone on to work in the Chinese employment sector, in Chinese-medium teaching, or in Chinese enterprises engaged in mining, wholesale, trading and construction or could have become self-employed as a petty trader. In this sector there would have been little or no chance of coming into personal contact with the other races, least of all with the Malays.

The 1950s, when my working life began, were leisurely and carefree days for most of us in government service. The development projects we worked on were fairly inconsequential. We did our work diligently enough, but much of it was routine. Racial friction did not seem to exist, certainly not within my circle of Malay, Chinese and Indian friends and colleagues. Instead, there was much camaraderie. There was frank and robust ribbing of each other's racial traits: Malays were "indolent and free-spending," Chinese were "cunning and grasping," Indians were "devious" and so on. No offence was meant or taken, it was just harmless teasing. In our immediate circle, remarks such as *"Keling balik India"* ("[You] Indians, go back to India"), *"Cina balik Tongsan"* ("[You] Chinese, go back to China") and *"Melayu balik kampung"* ("[You] Malays, go back to your village") were merely good-humoured banter and not the taunts they could, and did, become in the context of street quarrels.

Meanwhile, Malay nationalist stirrings, which had been making themselves felt for a long time, were propelling the country to *Merdeka*, or Independence. This came to pass in 1957, but Independence did not break our habit of deference to the old colonial master, and we were still contented to accept the British as our superiors. I was made particularly conscious of that habit by an incident—I will call it my first "race incident"—that took place soon after Independence.

It involved my boss and his boss. My boss was a fiftyish Indian. During the Japanese Occupation of Malaya, he was made the equivalent of State Engineer, the top post in the state. Then, with the end of the war, the British returned, and he was relegated to his old position in the District, a position seven or eight ranks below. His boss was English and barely half his age. One morning, I was helping my Indian boss to do "mustering"—marking the attendance of workers—when his English boss appeared. My boss greeted him by taking off his cork hat and folding it under his armpit, and, standing almost at attention, he addressed the young man as "Sir."

Now I greatly admired my boss, whom I thought an able officer, and whom I looked upon as a father figure to myself. To see a senior officer and gentleman like him having to behave so deferentially to a young white man was unsettling, to say the least. Of course, the scene was a commonplace in those colonial days, the norm as it were. Nor could the British officer be faulted for the way he conducted himself: he was courteous and perfectly "normal." Yet I thought: "Something is not right."

In the early 1960s, I left the government to work for myself. One of the things I tried my hand at was the spare parts business. The country was already independent but the colonial government practice of buying spare parts from the invariably British local agent was still in place. For the agent this was a cushy monopoly, a colonial legacy that had survived the departure of the British. With the help of old colleagues and by offering cheaper prices, we managed to make some inroads into that monopoly and make good money despite our lower margins.

One day, the British boss of the local agent came to see me. He said I had been selling spurious spare parts to his customers and I should desist. But as he was aware that I was carrying some stock, he wouldn't mind my selling that, but thereafter there was to be no more business. Otherwise he could make life difficult for me. All said in a civilised and not unfriendly manner. I listened incredulously and thought, "This white man is still talking like *Tuan* ("Master") almost ten years after *Merdeka*! I will show him!" This was my second "race incident."

I then got involved in the housing development business. In the early days of that business, getting approval for projects was fairly straightforward—only a question of dealing with the local authorities or the planning and land office. But with the launching of the NEP, land matters in the 1970s came increasingly under the control of politicians and the rules became progressively less precise. I have more to say about the NEP later, but suffice it to note at this stage that the policy was aimed at changing the ethnic pattern of economic power through measures favouring Malays. The rules became less precise because race had entered the picture.

I happened to be involved in a case where I had sold houses on a freehold basis only to be told by the state authorities that approval for subdivision would not be given unless I agreed to surrender the title in exchange for leasehold. It was a case of over-zealous politicians using administrative means to deny a landowner of his legal rights, at a time when it was *de rigueur* for a Malay politician to block Chinese business. The case eventually went to court, though I had been reluctant to resort to litigation. I won the case, but for years afterwards was blackballed for the arrogance and impertinence I had supposedly shown in taking the state government to court. It was my third "race incident," but the party involved was no longer white; it was brown.

As I progressed in business I became better acquainted with what might be called the Chinese merchant community. The majority of the members of this community were monolingual, Chinese-speaking, some fluent only in their own dialects. Many had had limited formal schooling. Some were born in China; others, the second-generation—that is to say, Malaya-born—Chinese, were raised in the immigrant Chinese merchant culture.

These men were the dominant players in the food, construction, mining, rubber and wholesale sectors. In the

1960s, they were still the movers and shakers of Malaysian business. They were immigrant Chinese businessmen of the old school, the sort to make their business deals in their clubs, or in the local hotels where they gathered most afternoons to gamble and play mahjong.

During the pre-NEP days, if you heard any mention of the Malays at all in their conversation, it was the usual light-hearted remark about their general incompetence. There were already government measures to give aspiring Malay entrepreneurs a leg up, but these measures were modest and any expectations the Malays might have had of their government helping them to succeed in business were not realised. "The Malays can't do it," was what you heard the Chinese merchants say in their clubs. Or else it was clichés like "They spend before they earn," and "They are not willing to work."

Then came the NEP, in the initial stages of which Chinese businesses were increasingly required to make room for Malay participation. The Malay presence became rather intrusive, and the Chinese began to think the Malays a nuisance. The comments changed, and what you heard now was, "They want too much," "They are greedy," or "They are corrupt." Malay participation was put down to government favouritism and set-asides. Such set-asides were thought to be ill- or unfairly-gotten advantages which did for the Malays what the Malays could not do for themselves. This was in the 1970s, some ten years before the NEP bore fruit and resulted in the emergence of serious Malay business entities. In those years I only ever heard them speak of the predicament of the Chinese under the NEP, never about the Malay dilemma.

If one spent any time in the company of these Chinese merchants, one would soon hear about bribery. To make a deal, one heard, the Chinese would often have to bribe someone. That someone could be of any colour; the payments, I soon learned, transcended all racial barriers. Kickbacks were offered regardless of whether the recipients were white, yellow, brown or black, or whether they were managers, or officials or even family trustees.

Lest I give the impression that I spent a great deal of my time with these merchants, I should add that the Chinese I mostly kept company with were the urban English-speaking ones, mainly wage earners, government servants, professionals or fledgling businessmen like myself. When I mixed with this group, it was as if I had a distinct existence. As a group we were culturally non-combative, by and large apolitical, and not as commercially acquisitive as the merchants, whose capital and skills we did not possess. Later our group would expand to include Malays. On the whole we were modest in our expectations in the 1960s, our concerns revolving around jobs and careers. In the 1970s, these concerns shifted towards job and promotion prospects, and access to tertiary education.

The distinctions between myself and the merchants illustrate the many distinctions that can be observed within the Chinese community. I have already mentioned the division according to the language of education (Chinese or English) and to the place of birth or generation (China-born or locally born). On which side of the divide we fall influences the amount of cultural baggage we carry, and this in turn affects how we perceive our situation in Malaysia.

Of course cultural baggage is not the only thing which influences our perceptions. How we have fared in this country, individually and as a group, also affects the way we see

Malaysia and the Malays. And we would hardly be human beings if emotions did not colour our perceptions. Within the Chinese community, I find, there are wide disparities in perception. It is to examine these perceptions and, it has to be admitted, to question those which diverge from my own that I attempt this book. The exercise will I hope raise some issues for further airing and debate.

Am I a heretic? Writing this book, I run the risk of being condemned as a traitor or a racist. I find it awkward to question the long-held beliefs of the Malaysian Chinese—a feeling akin to betrayal. Few Chinese will be unacquainted with this feeling, which comes of the cultural baggage most of us carry. Perhaps all I can do is to quote from *The Malay Dilemma*: "The publication of this book is not calculated to endear the writer to any particular section of the Malaysians. Indeed, it is most likely to cause despondency among some, and severe resentment among most others. No apologies are offered. What I have written is written with sincerity."

I am sure my views will draw detractors from all sides. However, I can claim to be true of heart. I have no political axe to grind, nor do I harbour any political agenda, and there is certainly no money in this. As for posterity, I have always thought it overcrowded with names already, and in any case any Dilemma it remembers will be *The Malay Dilemma*! It is my hope that this book will be read, and not only read but discussed, because if I have any purpose it is to encourage debate and reflection, which in turn would help us Chinese to see our way forward in Malaysia more clearly.

CHAPTER 2

POLITICAL BACKDROP

I WENT INTO my own background in the last chapter because in thinking about race relations, which is the subject of this book, one is bound to be influenced by one's family upbringing, education, values and experiences; and those who agree or disagree with my views should know, as they say in America, "where I am coming from."

Having summarised my personal history, I should now sketch the nation's. My life has spanned the colonial, Independence, post-Independence, NEP and post-NEP periods. To look back over this fifty-year span is to be astonished by the enormous progress Malaysia has made. Just a glance at *The Malay Dilemma* the career of its author is enough to give one a sense of how far things have changed.

Mahathir was born in the northern state of Kedah, the son of a humble school teacher. He studied at the local English school and then went on to study medicine at the University of Malaya in Singapore (then part of colonial Malaya). There, in the same class, he met Siti Hasmah Mohd. Ali, who was to become his wife. They were among the five

Malays in a class of seventy. Upon graduation in 1953, he entered government service, then left to go into private medical practice.

Mahathir had shown a keen interest in community matters since his school days and as a young man often wrote articles for publication in newspapers. He is fond of describing himself as "a politician who became a doctor." He had been a member of UMNO (United Malays National Organisation), Malaya's first, and today's ruling, political party since its inception; but in 1969, shortly after the racial riots, he was expelled from it by the Tunku (as Tunku Abdul Rahman was affectionately known to all).

To know why, read the chapter headed "What Went Wrong?" in *The Malay Dilemma*. Here Mahathir asks why the riots happened and gives his answers, each one a sharp criticism of the government, straight from the shoulder. They were no doubt the very criticisms which he had voiced to the party leaders and which had proved too much for the Tunku, who had sacked him.

"Obviously a lot went wrong," Mahathir writes, then goes on to list, pulling no punches, all the mistakes made by the government. To begin with, he says, the government "started off on the wrong premise." It assumed that there was racial harmony between the Chinese and the Malays. It assumed that "the Chinese were only interested in business and acquisition of wealth, and that the Malays wished only to become Government servants." These are ridiculous assumptions, he writes.

Which they indeed are. The absurdity is clear to us now, but, incredible as it may seem in hindsight, it was not so clear then, or at least not to those Malay and Chinese leaders who entered upon the early years of Malaysian nationhood with the understanding (with a kind of "bargain") that the political predominance of the Malays would not be challenged so long as the Chinese were allowed to pursue unimpeded their traditional commercial and industrial activities. This was tantamount to telling the Chinese that they could go on being the haves so long as they agreed to leave the running of the country to the have-nots. Put this way, the absurdity of the "bargain" becomes instantly apparent. That it seems patently obvious to us now is perhaps a measure of how far things have changed since the time Mahathir was banished from UMNO and branded a Malay chauvinist for suggesting just that. In a way, his words make perhaps even more interesting reading now than they did in their day.

He was brought back into the fold in 1972 by Abdul Razak, who succeeded the Tunku as prime minister. To the departing British, the Tunku had seemed the best man to lead the new nation. He was the scion of a royal family; he had spent unduly long years studying Law in England (and having a grand time while he was at it). But against the backdrop of changing times he now appeared overly Anglophile and pro-Chinese, and insufficiently "Malay" and Muslim. In a campaign to discredit him in 1969, his political enemies put up a photograph of the Tunku at a Chinese dinner using a pair of chopsticks, with a suckling pig in the middle of the table superimposed on the picture. No attack on his relaxed attitudes towards race and religion could be more stinging.

There was no love lost between the Tunku and Mahathir. Interviewed after a heart attack late in life, the Tunku said with a chuckle that two doctors had saved his life—his cardiologist, and Dr. Mahathir, the latter because, as the Tunku put it, "I wanted to live so that I can fight him." It is worth spending a few paragraphs looking into this animosity, because in it are entwined many of the issues raised in this book.

The Tunku, interestingly enough, also originated in Kedah; indeed the headmaster of his first school—to which, in princely fashion, he was carried every morning on the shoulders of his retainer—was Mahathir's father.

Shortly after the May 1969 riots, he received, he later related, "a scurrilous letter from Dr. Mahathir .... It was a letter the likes of which I had never seen before in all my political career, and the most unlikely communication I would have expected to get from a man who had always put himself forward, at least outwardly, as a staunch supporter of the party even though he disagreed with some of the policies." Among other things, the four-page letter typed in Malay (which I believe remains banned till this day), demanded the resignation of the Tunku as prime minister. Mahathir, the Tunku huffed, belonged to the group of men usually referred to as the "ultras" or, "as they preferred to be known, the intellectuals."

It was not that the Tunku was unaware of the Malay predicament; indeed he had summed it up well enough when he said, "In the economic life of the nation foreigners got all the advantages and privileges with the enterprising Chinese coming second. The Malays had no share in the business life of the country. Their lot was indeed a dismal one because they led a hand-to-mouth existence. For too long they were repeatedly told, and believed, that the colonial government were their benefactors and so they lived on in ignorance and quiet contentment." But his views on what means should be used to better the Malay lot were considered outdated by the younger and more assertive intellectuals, who wanted a new order of things.

The Tunku was a man of his time and Mahathir a man of his. Those who were acquainted with the Tunku knew there was a seriousness behind that easygoing exterior. Today we forget how enormous a change he made in the life of the nation when he persuaded the British to grant Independence. His wit, his charm, the very fact that at one point in the negotiations he asked for tickets to watch Arsenal play in the FA Cup final were just the qualities to appeal to the British.

Decolonisation was but the first step in the creation of the Malaysian nation: there were the negotiations for the "merger" of Malaya and Singapore, and for the federation of Sabah and Sarawak to form a united Malaysia. It was the Tunku who welded the new federation together, and who, faced with irreconcilable differences with Lee Kuan Yew in 1965, asked Singapore to quit Malaysia—in the interest, as he put it in a letter, of "the security and peace of Malaysia as a whole." He remained firm in his decision, and Malaysia was able to weather the crisis without pulling further apart.

He was the leader the Malays needed at that particular juncture of Malaysian history. As a friend of his who became a member of his government put it: "The Malays required a sincere man. We knew from experience that Tunku possessed that quality. He was not all that smart but we knew he would make a sincere and a real leader."

Yet while his patrician, humane, old-style *laissez-faire* politics served the Malays well at the time, what the Malays also needed was a "new deal." And that "new deal" could only be given to them by a new brand of politics and a new type of politician. The fall of Tunku and the rise of Mahathir marked the change from a gradualist, hands-off approach favouring multiracial compromise to an approach favouring far stronger state intervention and Malay-first policies. The transition, you might say, marked a Malay coming of age.

Brought back into the mainstream of Malaysian politics by Abdul Razak, Mahathir was given the ministerial portfolio for Education. Abdul Razak came to be called the Father of National Development but a better title would have been Father of Malay Nationalism. A very experienced and astute politician, he was able to advance Malay interests and still command Chinese support.

It was under his aegis that the NEP was implemented. In essence, the NEP's aim was to increase, within twenty years of its inception, the Malay share of the nation's corporate assets from just under 2 per cent to 30. At the time foreign interests had the largest slice of the corporate cake, but the Chinese cut was, at a little under 30 per cent, not inconsiderable either. The Malay increase, though, was not meant to be at the expense of any other group's portion. The idea was that the whole cake should get larger even as it was being divided up differently; to use the official phraseology, the NEP was to work towards a two-part goal: one, the restructuring of Malaysian society to correct economic imbalance so as to reduce and eventually eliminate the identification of race with economic function; and two, to eradicate poverty by raising income levels and increasing employment opportunities for all Malaysians, irrespective of race. In other words, the pie would grow bigger, it would be cut up more evenly, and everyone—whether Malay, Chinese or Indian—would get a larger slice.

About halfway through the NEP's term, Mahathir became prime minister. Abdul Razak had died in office in 1976, and his deputy and successor, Hussein Onn, had resigned for health reasons in 1981. Hussein had a reputation for being scrupulously honest and fair-minded, and his appointment as prime minister, at a time of increasing Malay assertiveness under the NEP, reassured the non-Malay community.

He had earlier sprung a surprise by choosing Mahathir to be his deputy—a surprise because Mahathir was known to be a rebel. It has also been noted that Mahathir was the first prime minister not to have been educated in Britain, the first not of aristocratic birth, the first not trained as a lawyer, and the first who did not play golf.

He seemed a man impatient to get things done, stressing efficiency, the work ethic and discipline. "We are not workaholics," he once said, "though we think we should be." He insisted on civil servants "clocking in" and arriving at the office on time. In the past civil servants had made it their business to regulate and police the private sector; his brainchild, the concept of "Malaysia Incorporated," reorientated them towards working with the private sector in the nation's larger interests. He moved the country into heavy industry and pushed its industrialisation into higher gear.

Then he took on the aristocratic ruling class (the sultans), and also the advanced Western nations. He has not baulked at ending the sultans' privileges, such as their immunity from prosecution. His adoption of the Look East Policy implied both a recognition of the lessons to be learned from Japan and South Korea, and a criticism of the values, hypocrisy and declining standards of the West. The double standards by which the world's richest nations judge other countries periodically come in for an earful from him.

One does not envy any Malaysian prime minister his job. Running the country requires a consummate player in the game of political balance. Quite apart from the potential disunity implied by the racial diversity, there was, and there continues to be, the need to tap the forces of progress and modernity without offending against Islamic sensibilities and alienating devout Muslims. The demands of rural traditionalists have to be reconciled with the wishes of forward-looking urbanites. A delicate equilibrium has to be maintained here, a feat of co-option performed there. Malaysia is an immensely complex society, far more complex than, say, Singapore, a country with which it has often been compared and contrasted. Few people would disagree with me, I think, when I say that it is greatly to the Malay leadership's credit that Malaysians enjoy a climate of prosperity and political stability today.

Mahathir first entered national consciousness as a nationalist to the Malays and a racist to the non-Malays. Today, he remains a nationalist to the Malays but, among a growing number of them, he is not only nationalist but secular as well, a taunt calculated to cause disaffection among them against him. On the other hand, I doubt if many non-Malays these days think of him as a racist. Yet, if over time, perceptions about him have changed, the strength of his convictions have not nor the vigour and cool singlemindedness with which he pursues them. He does not shy away from confronting issues, however controversial, and people, however powerful, that come in the way.

As a result, he has established a reputation of combativeness, which his demeanour belies. He is gentle of manner, softly spoken and always polite—even as he throws barbs at his opponents or questioners, it is always done in a soft and even tone. In interviews by the U.S. business print and television media, being bluntly questioned about corruption in his government, cronyism, nepotism, etc., he maintained his composure, responding to the provocation in his mild gentle manner with answers like "give me proof," "I have nothing to do with my children's business." Looking at the man, I am reminded of Brutus in Shakespeare's *Julius Caesar* who, when accused of plotting against Caesar, responded "I am armed so strong in honesty that your threats passed me like idle winds which I respect not."

Such has been the career of the author of *The Malay Dilemma*. It is interesting to note that *The Malay Dilemma* remained banned until 1983, more than ten years after Mahathir joined the Cabinet and two years after he became Prime Minister. Unusual for a sitting Prime Minister, he has continued to write and publish mostly on race, national, social and economic matters—*The Way Forward, The Challenge* and *A New Deal for Asia* are some of his recent writings. He appears willing to put his thoughts and convictions in print for all to scrutinise.

For all that, Mahathir's deep-seated concern for the viability of his race has persisted in the face of all the advancement made by the Malays over the period of the NEP. It is worthwhile quoting the concluding lines of his last opening address to the UMNO general assembly as president in June 2003, which betrays the poignancy of his emotions over his dreams, hopes and fears for the Malay race. To quote: "This is the last time that I can deliver the speech to officially open the UMNO general assembly. I crave your pardon if I took too much time. I truly wish to repay the party, which had given me opportunities to realise my ideas on restoring the honour of my race and people, to help to progress them and my country. It is not for me to say whether I have succeeded or not. The people and history will judge and determine whether my service was good or bad. I value very much the support of UMNO, the Malays and other *Bumiputeras* and the people of Malaysia and I am grateful and I thank them all. I crave your pardon for the mistakes and wrongs that I have committed during the length of my leadership of this blessed party. Allah be Praised, for having given His insignificant slave this opportunity. I pray to Him to protect this, my race from the bad qualities and make them a people who are successful and honoured, who submit fully to all that our holy religion has taught us, to make them work hard, that You may protect and bring success to our people in order to become the model to the Muslim *ummah*, the people who submit to all your injunctions, Oh Allah, Amin."

Brief as it is, my sketch of his career is enough, though, to show that there is far more to his agenda than the furtherance of Malay interests. But whether or not history will judge him a great reformer is not the immediate concern of my sketch, which is really by way of providing background. In the next chapter I want to narrow my focus and turn from the backdrop of political developments to the evolution of Chinese-Malay relations over time.

CHAPTER 3

SEEDS OF DISCORD

M*ERDEKA* might have signalled a fresh start, if there were such things as fresh starts. There aren't, of course, when it comes to race. Events in the past had implanted volatile elements in the racial patchwork of Malaysian society. I am no historian, but it doesn't take a historian to know what those events were. To begin with, there was the surge of Chinese nationalism in the first decades of this century.

I have a close friend whom I have known since high school. His excellent Cantonese and Mandarin reflect the years of Chinese schooling he had had before he went on to receive an English-medium education. I had occasion to see him for lunch recently, and to hear him reminisce about his youth. Looking back at one point upon his early school days in the mid- to late-1940s, he began to talk about the nationalism of his fellow-Chinese pupils.

He was not himself politically engaged, but it was all around him, that current of China-centred patriotism endemic to Chinese-medium schools throughout Malaya. You could, like my friend, stay aloof from it, but you couldn't avoid it, not if you were in a Chinese-medium school.

Much of what my friend was saying was outside my own experience, something that one couldn't really relate to if one was at an English-medium school. China was the model for those Chinese-medium schools, just as Britain was, I suppose, for the English-language ones. Such being the case, I should clearly have found it harder to resist becoming a Chinese chauvinist if I had gone to a Chinese-language school. We all know that education is a form of indoctrination. Malaya was no different from other British colonies in having many of the ruled taking on the attitudes of the rulers and looking down on monolingual Chinese speakers. Similarly, the products of Chinese schools tended to disdain those whose Chineseness had been diluted by English education; in the eyes of these people, to study at an English school was to be distanced from the Chinese cultural heritage. They disparagingly referred to the English-educated as *er maozi*, "second-class person."

The Chinese nationalism of which my friend spoke that afternoon was naturally strongest during periods when China was invaded (by Japan, for example), or when it suffered humiliation at the hands of Western powers. In fact, you could say that from about 1920 to the 1950s, Chinese patriotic sentiments abroad were a transplantation of patriotic emotions at home.

Those sentiments revolved around the theme of national salvation in the face of foreign incursion. There was a feeling that one went to school not only to acquire the qualifications to earn a living, but to contribute to the regeneration of one's mother country.

You often hear it said that the immigrant Chinese are not interested in politics, only in making money. The truth of the matter is that they are by no means uninterested in politics, far from it; it is just that, until about the 1950s, they were interested in the affairs of their mother country to the exclusion almost of every other kind of politics. Both the two rival parties of China—the Kuomintang (or Nationalists) and the Chinese Communist Party—had front organisations and followers in Malaya, and the struggle between the two in Malaya mirrored their struggle in China. Contemporary Malay observers took a dim view of this, and did not mince their words when, voicing their disgruntlement in the press, they told the Chinese to keep China's politics out of Malaya.

Of course not all Malayan Chinese were equally riveted by China's politics. It did not impinge on the English-educated, who probably had little inkling of the political goings-on in the Chinese community. Then there were people like my friend who did take an interest in Chinese affairs, but who in no way identified with China's destiny. That left the activists, the most political of all the different types of Malayan Chinese. They were the ones whose minds were fixed on China, and who discounted local issues or Malay politics as having no bearing on themselves.

Many of them took up arms in resistance when the Japanese invaded Malaya in 1941. The war gave impetus to the communist movement, and the Malayan Communist Party (MCP) won a lot of kudos for leading the anti-Japanese guerrilla resistance. Communism had been introduced by Chinese immigrants from China, and although the MCP succeeded in raising a Malay regiment in the state of Pahang, the party was nine-tenths Chinese.

As fighters of the Japanese, the communists had started out on the same side as the British, but it wasn't long after the end of the war before they began showing their true anti-imperialist colours and started waging a guerrilla war against the British—the Emergency (1948-1960).

I shall come back to the Emergency, but first I want to return to my earlier point about past events implanting volatile elements in Malaysian society. The Japanese Occupation was definitely one of those events. During that period, the Malays were pitted against the Chinese as never before. China being their number one enemy, the Japanese made sure that of all the races in Malaya the Chinese would be the most brutally treated. The Malays were persuaded to collaborate, brought in to fill administrative jobs and to swell the ranks of the police force. And these Malay policemen were the people the Japanese used in their anti-Chinese operations. It would be strange if such actions did not create bad blood between the two races.

After the Japanese surrender, the Chinese exacted their revenge. Old scores were settled in bloody racial clashes. The communist guerrillas emerged from the jungle, and entered Chinese villages and Malay *kampungs* to seek out and punish collaborators. They were cruel and ferocious in their methods, and the Malays retaliated. According to one historical account, a *jihad* (Holy War) was waged against the Chinese by groups of the *Sufi tarekat* (brotherhood) in half a dozen states, and large numbers of deaths resulted. In the reprisals and counter-reprisals, neither Chinese nor Malays were spared the worst of racial acrimony.

Against such a background of racial polarisation, it was inevitable that the Malay and Indian recruits into the communist guerrilla army should quickly quit it, leaving the MCP with an undiluted Chinese identity. The "Chinese Party," it became known to the Malays from that time on. The Malays formed the bulk of the security forces and did most of the fighting. How could they not feel that the Chinese were a menace to Malaya?

The communists had a base of support in the "squatters," rural Chinese occupying the jungle fringes. The British authorities made it a part of their counter-guerrilla campaign to resettle these squatters in fortified and defended compounds called New Villages. Finding their sources of food and supplies drying up, the communists began to prey on the Indians and the Malays. The violence and intimidation that the *kampung* Malays suffered at the hands of these Chinese guerrillas widened the breach between the two races. The Emergency was eventually brought to an end, but not before it had added to the legacy of racial resentment.

Yet it would be unfair to leave the reader with the impression that Chinese-Malay relations were embittered only by Chinese nationalism, Japanese Occupation, and the Malayan Emergency. The picture is, of course, much more complicated than that. There were the British, for a start. Nowadays it is a commonplace to blame the colonial master for the troubles of an ex-colony. I think that the apportioning of blame is best left to historians and social scientists. I am neither a historian nor a social scientist, but like every other Malaysian whose life has spanned the colonial and post-Independence periods, I can see for myself how British policies impacted on interracial relations.

The Chinese had been trading and settling in Southeast Asia long before the British came, but their influx into the

Malay Peninsula did not become a flood until the onset of the colonial age. What the imperialists did was to turn the place into an open frontier of opportunity. Immigrants from India and Ceylon were also encouraged to come, but their numbers were not nearly as large as those of the Chinese.

Nor did the British come only as conquerors and rulers; many came as capitalists and merchants. Profound economic changes were ushered in, creating opportunities for entrepreneurs, middlemen, retail traders, and wage labourers. Those opportunities were eagerly seized by the incoming Chinese.

This was a familiar pattern throughout Southeast Asia, but peninsular Malaya stood out from all other parts of the region in the scale of its Chinese immigration. A staggering number of Chinese poured in between the early nineteenth century and World War II. Most came for a time and then returned to China, but the pool of remaining Chinese was continuously replenished with fresh immigration. By the end of the war, there were two and a half million Chinese in Malaya, comprising 38 per cent of the total population, of whom 64 per cent were locally born.

It had been British policy to keep the doors open to all comers, until it was realised—and that realisation came as something of a shock in 1931—that the Malays were outnumbered in their own country by non-Malays: the census that year showed that Chinese and Indians made up as much as 53.2 per cent of the population, while the Malays were only 44.7. The Malays were in serious danger of being overrun by aliens. Alarmed, the British decreed restrictions on further Chinese immigration, but this was a case of shutting the stable door after the horse has bolted.

The trouble was that the British had their own dilemma too. Their ultimate end was the advancement of their own interests, and in pursuing this end, for which they needed the services of the Chinese, they could not help but advance the interests of the Chinese as well. But how to do all this without disadvantaging the Malays? How to increase their own fortunes and, by extension, those of the Chinese, and at the same time shield the Malays from Chinese encroachment? That was their dilemma, one that was never resolved.

The Chinese, concentrated in the ports and towns, stood to gain far more than the Malays from the development of the country. Grounded in traditional agricultural society, the Malays were almost completely left out of the currents of economic and urban expansion. They were left high and dry, you might say. As for the Malay sultans, it has to be said that many were conservative rulers who would not have welcomed an interruption to the traditional, tranquil way of life of their peasant subjects. But in being spared the disruptiveness of capitalist development, the Malay peasant was also denied the benefits of that experience.

That the Malays kept to their villages suited the British well enough. It meant that there were always people to work the land and produce the food (particularly rice). Disturbing the natural rhythms of rural Malay society might raise a political dust and the British didn't want that. As they saw it, they were there to protect the Malays and preserve their culture, not uproot them from their *kampungs* and make townies out of them. In any case, it was a part of English character to idealise life in the countryside. The tiller of land no doubt struck the British, with their romantic ideas about the Noble Savage, as a man of far greater dignity than the pedlar.

To sum up, under the British the different races were divided by employment and geography: the Malays growing rice and fishing while living in their villages; the Chinese concentrating on tin mining and commerce and filling the towns; the Indians working in rubber plantations or in transport or, in the case of the better educated, as government clerks.

The rural character of Malay livelihood was consolidated by the British creation of Malay land reservations, which were introduced to protect the Malays from losing their plots to the land-hungry rubber industry and to safeguard Malay patrimony.

All along the British recognised that the Malays had special rights because they were the host population; they themselves owed their authority to the traditional recognition of the sultans. Where the Malays were concerned, the British were paternalistic and protective. The intention was to help the Malays, but the consequence was perhaps to discourage them from helping themselves. To protect someone is often to surround him with a gentle environment that does not extract his best.

Under British policy, the Chinese were allowed limited access to the administrative or executive ranks of the public service, whereas Malays were trained and recruited into the colonial bureaucracy. Did this hamper the Chinese, or did it drive them, as similar restrictions did the Jews of Europe, all the more strongly towards success in private business? Mahathir remarks in his book that while the British carved out a Malay reservation within the town limits of Kuala Lumpur, "elsewhere, especially where British rule was more direct, the Malays found no champion at all," implying that the British should have championed the Malay cause, but did not. Yet in another part of his book, he observes that what galvanised the Malays into organising themselves in the aftermath of the Japanese Occupation was the discovery that they could no longer count on the British to champion their cause. It was the shock of finding themselves abandoned to their fate that made the Malays take their fate into their own hands. If such things could ever be dated, it was from that moment that Malay nationalism flowered. So should the British have done more for the Malays, when all is said and done, or should they have done less? It is hard to know. As Edmund Burke said, "He that wrestles with us strengthens our nerves, and sharpens our skill. Our antagonist is our helper."

The Malay shock was in connection with the British plan to form the Malayan Union, a first step on the road to Malayan Independence. This would have destroyed the basis of the Malays' protected position. Among other things, the union would have made citizens of more than 80 per cent of the Chinese and 75 per cent of the Indians. That was something the Malays simply could not countenance, alerted as they were to the threat of being overwhelmed by non-Malay immigrants. In their uncharacteristically assertive opposition to the union (an opposition led by the newly formed UMNO), they found a unity they had never known before.

The Malayan Union was aborted. But the whole exercise had succeeded in raising the consciousness of rights in all the three main communities. "Special rights," "equal rights"—the arguments about these marked the way to self-government. Many Chinese realised it was time they involved themselves more deeply in the politics of their adopted country, if they wanted a stake in the soon-to-be-born Malayan nation. But they lacked the Malays' unity. Still, the need to develop a communal party, one that was decidedly not communist, spurred them to form the Malayan Chinese Association (MCA).

In the future nation, the separate racial communities would no longer be held together by an alien colonial force. What would replace British authority? In the end, what was concocted was a form of multiracial power sharing, a Malay-Chinese alliance that was later joined by the Indians, who had organised themselves into the Malayan Indian Congress (MIC) and who now completed the communal triangle. The agreement to the communal alliance revolved around a trade-off: special rights for the Malays, plus the acceptance of Malay as the sole official and national language, in exchange for citizenship for the Chinese and Indians. (I should add by way of a footnote that in the aftermath of the race riots in 1969, Abdul Razak adroitly brought the opposition parties into the alliance to form the Barisan Nasional, the National Front coalition.)

There were two aspects to the Malay's "special rights." One was historical: colonial rule had been subject to the treaties signed with the Malay sultans, so that, if the departing British made Malaya over to any sovereign power, it would be to Malay sovereign power. There could be no argument about that: the British had all along considered Malaya to be Malay. The Malays were special by virtue of their status as "sons of the soil" (*Bumiputera*).

The other side to their specialness was more controversial. Here specialness was defined by need. The Malays were to be given special treatment, by reserving quotas of entry for them, in areas such as government employment, trade and business opportunities, education and land rights because materially they lagged so far behind the other races. The special treatment, in other words, was predicated on their special needs. Their right to such special treatment was to be enshrined in the new Constitution.

To give to the Malays, the other races were assured, was not to take from the non-Malays. But the Chinese were not assured. Malay special rights rankled with them then, and still rankle with them today. As I mentioned earlier, among the Chinese merchants I came into contact with, there was a concern for the Chinese predicament but never for the Malay dilemma. This, in my view, is wrong.

CHAPTER 4

THE MALAY DILEMMA REVISITED

I AM TOLD by an Indian friend of mine that when it comes to the race question in Malaysia, not only are my views wrong but the whole premise on which they rest is mistaken. To start off on the wrong premise, he says, is to end up with the wrong conclusion. He does not accept that premise; and nor do many Malaysian Chinese.

What is my premise? It is that the Malays are the hosts, and we Chinese and Indians the guests. We came in such large numbers that it is no wonder the word "annexation" has been used of us. Indeed it could be said that the Malays allowed us to pitch a tent and we ended up taking possession of their land. Still, if we had ended up as coolies, I don't think we would have had any "Malay dilemma." But instead we prospered and came to dominate the mainstream of Malaysian life—in business, in the professions, in the universities—and we occupied all the major towns. If I were Malay I would not have allowed such a state of affairs to go unchallenged: my sense of pride and honour would not allow it. Malay self-esteem would require that, having rid themselves of the colonial master, they wrested economic power from the Chinese.

This is how the Malays have felt and will continue to feel. That feeling antedated the appearance of *The Malay Dilemma*, which merely made explicit how the Malays viewed their situation all along. Whatever arguments we may choose to defend the legitimacy of our position—citizens' rights, democratic practice—will not alter this view, for it is fortified by emotion, self-esteem and also need. I have often asked my non-Malay friends, "If the Malays had come to occupy India and China in a similar manner, how do you imagine the Indians and Chinese would feel? How would they have responded to these intruders? What would they have done?"

As I see it, the Malay bid for economic parity is not only natural but just. Any people in their position would, if they could, do what they did. My acknowledging this makes it easier for me to understand and accept their claim to a reasonable share of the economy and their efforts to regain their pride; and when I look at the immigrant experience in other countries, I am persuaded that it is also in my interest to do so.

I am persuaded that Malaysia has found a viable solution to the problems of racial/economic division. All this makes me feel thankful for having been raised a Malaysian. We have now had decades of Independence and the NEP behind us. If, in that period, the government made a hash of the economy or of race relations, then obviously I would not feel the same way. But it has delivered the goods and at what I believe is an acceptable price.

I also look at the lot of Chinese and Indian migrants to other countries and that of those who had stayed home. This is enough to make me feel thankful that I am here and not there. To take the Chinese first, think of those Boat People (many of them of Chinese origin) forced to flee Vietnam; think of Cambodia, where the Chinese were killed or driven away; think of Indonesia, with its persecution and expulsion of the Chinese; think of the Philippines, where for so long the Chinese were effectively denied citizenship. Of course there is Thailand, where the Chinese are said to suffer no discrimination, but that is because they are assimilated to Thai society and have in a way given up their Chinese identity.

Farther afield, in the U.S., Canada and Australia, their history is a chronicle of struggles against exclusion, victimisation and indignity. And as for those Malaysian Chinese who migrated to these countries in the years following Independence, most of them professionals and people armed with some capital, economic success has not come as easily as it has to those who stayed at home. If many came back to Malaysia in the early and mid-1990s, it was not just because these countries were in recession. It was also because of the lack of opportunity, the indirect discrimination, the so-called "glass ceiling" and the stiffer competition.

I compare where I am today with where I would be if, instead of coming here, my parents had remained in China. Or if the Malays had said to the Chinese, "Heh, you *balik Tongsan*" ("Why don't you go back to China?") and repatriated us. A migrant from the Indian subcontinent, when he looks back at India and Sri Lanka, would surely arrive at the same conclusion, that Malaysia has been the better place for him than his country of origin. In Sri Lanka Tamils and Sinhalese had lived together for two millennia without much hostility, but look at it now. Look at Fiji and East Africa, which have been so much less hospitable to their large Indian immigrant communities than Malaysia.

But I think I can see what my Indian friend is getting at when he tells me my premise is wrong. He wouldn't start from the same premise. I wouldn't presume to speak for him but I can fit him into a context, and that context tells one something about his starting point.

During colonial times, Indians with English education were recruited from India to work in supervisory and clerical positions. Today, a large proportion of the educated and successful Indians in Malaysia are professionals, particularly lawyers. Migrants from the Indian subcontinent are also over-represented in the trade union movement. In their approach to politics the professionals echo the Western intelligentsia, and they admire the Westminster system of government; the trade unionists, on the other hand, seek the adoption in Malaysia of industrial practices that reflect a "democratic socialist" ideal. On the whole the educated Indians are probably more comfortable with the Anglo-Saxon culture of individualism, a culture which stresses the rights of individual citizens and which rejects any suggestion that someone is to have greater or lesser rights because he belongs to a particular category. Malay privileges contradict one of the strands of this culture: the value attached to equal treatment.

My Indian friend would also reject my use of the word "annexation" for non-Malay migration to this country. Here I am reminded of a row reported in the press in early 1994 over whether or not the British colonisation of Australia could be termed an "invasion." The state premier of Queensland, Australia, ordered references to an "invasion" deleted from a textbook, causing an uproar among some academics and Aboriginals. The premier's argument was that there is a world of difference between the arrival of the British and what most people understand as an invasion. Others said the correction was necessary because the word "settlement," traditionally used by the history books, suggests that the British colonists who arrived in the 18th century did not take land from Australia's native Aboriginals.

All of us are where we are in the world today because of conquest and migration. Conquest is a costly business, usually involving sacrifice of life and, if the victory is to be sustained, an expenditure of resources to keep the conquered in continued subjugation. Migration does not involve such costs, or at least involves fewer costs. So if the British, Chinese and Malays were all seen to be contenders for the same territory, then by doing it through migration rather than conquest, the Chinese may be said to have gained their share at relatively little cost. They haven't even had to fight a war to get where they have in Malaysia. And while the British came for a time and then left, they stayed on and became permanent inhabitants.

As for making comparisons between the adopted country and the ancestral homeland, my Indian friend would not think that quite right either. In certain liberal circles in the West, it is not done to suggest that an immigrant is better off where he is than back home. To draw, as I do, a comparison between Malaysia and China (or India) would be to lay oneself open to accusations of what I am told is called the "new racism." Today, the American author James Truslow Adams, who made the following remark in the 1930s about the

American of African descent, would be thought guilty of "new racism": "The condition of the portion of that continent from which he came was one not only of savagery but of chronic warfare, quite irrespective of the activities of the slave traders. A Negro in his native land was liable at any moment to be attacked, captured, enslaved by other blacks, torn from his family, or killed and in some cases eaten. Would the 12,000,000 Negroes in the United States today prefer that their ancestors had never been enslaved and that therefore they themselves, if alive, should at this moment be living as savages or barbarians in the African jungle? Would a Du Bois [a famous black scholar and fighter for black rights] prefer to be head man to an African chief instead of a Harvard graduate, scholar and writer .... Would the coloured washerwoman I had in the North give up her comfortable house and her car, in which she motored her family to Virginia each summer, for the ancestral grass hut in the jungle?"

My Indian friend would not think it valid to compare the life of the black washerwoman in America (where she can live in a comfortable house and drive to Virginia every summer) with her life in Africa (where she will have a hut in the jungle). And he has a point. But nevertheless mine is that if I were that washerwoman I would feel grateful to be in America and not Africa. Similarly I cannot but feel a sense of gratitude for having been raised in Malaysia rather than China. But I find few Chinese or Indians recognising this dimension to the race debate.

Why don't they? Some Chinese dispute the fact that the land was the Malays' to begin with. Others say that it was the British who had opened the door to them, and their head start is owed to colonial policy. Yet others say that they have helped to develop the country and have contributed to its prosperity, so they have a rightful share in whatever is on offer.

One who exemplifies the first view is Lee Kuan Yew. On the eve of Singapore's separation from Malaysia, he cast doubt on the whole idea that the Malays were the natives of Malaya, and by doing so implied that the Chinese had as much right to be there as the Malays.

He questioned the basis of the Malay claim to Malaysia: "According to history," he said, "Malays began to migrate to Malaysia in noticeable numbers only about 700 years ago. Of the 39 per cent Malays in Malaysia today, about one-third are comparatively new immigrants like the secretary-general of UMNO, Dato' Syed Ja'afar Albar, who came to Malaya from Indonesia just before the war at the age of more than thirty. Therefore it is wrong and illogical for a particular racial group to think that they are more justified to be called Malaysians and that the others can become Malaysian only through their favour."

He scoffed at the idea that any Malay of the Malay Archipelago could be considered natives of Malaysia by virtue of their racial origin. Such a theory, he said, would permit Indonesia to infiltrate more than four and a half million Indonesians into the country, to have a plebiscite and win a popular mandate to take over Malaysia.

To me there has never been any question that Malaya belongs to the Malays and not to the Chinese or Indians. As was mentioned in an earlier chapter, the British had all along recognised Malay sovereignty and that if they returned power to anyone, it would be to the Malays.

In any event, arguing over "who was there first" doesn't get you anywhere. We are past all that now: the Malays are in command and that's all there is to it. Arguing about it is not really very fruitful because if being there first really counted, then Aboriginals would be running Australia and Taiwan, Native Americans (once called Red Indians) would be governing the United States, and Malays Singapore. Some nation states are ethnically and culturally rooted, but many are not. The boundaries which define us as nation states have been drawn or redrawn for reasons other than the delimitation of coherent ethnic groups.

Then there is the argument that "you did not let us in, the British did." In answer to this, I would ask if this doesn't, in a way, make us "accessories after the fact?" It is widely agreed that American Indians and Australian Aboriginals were wronged by the white colonisers. Suppose large numbers of alien migrants had followed these colonisers into America and Australia. Are they to be absolved entirely from blame?

Another Chinese argument goes like this: "It was no thanks to you that we made good; it was thanks to our own efforts. Such advantages as we gained over you were gained under colonial rule. Not that the British favoured us particularly. Our prosperity was the side effect rather than the intention of British policy; British-sponsored migration was underpinned by the colonial need for cheap and reliable labour, and we provided that labour. The British used us all right, but in the process of using us they included us in the developing economy, and it so happened that we benefited from being part of that economy. We did not 'choose' Malaya—many of our forbears were brought in as coolies who had no idea where they were being taken to when they were shipped from China. Nor is it our fault that, at the time of our arrival, you were out of the running and we were in, so that we raced ahead of you. You did not 'allow' us to get ahead of you; you were not in a position to allow anything."

That is certainly one way of looking at it, but it's not mine. It is not mine because it starts from the premise that it's every man for himself, and while I have no quarrel with the belief that it's every man for himself, I would suggest that in this case we didn't start from here. We need to remind ourselves that at the time of Independence Malaysia was in no position to indulge in a free-for-all.

How could it be when the starting line was not the same for everyone; when some people were better placed than others to begin with? The Chinese gained from his inclusion in the developing capitalist economy; the Malay lost by virtue of his exclusion. Are we then to say to the Malay, "Too bad," and leave it at that? Will the Malay accept that? Indeed will he allow it? Isn't it incumbent upon us to take cognisance of Malay feelings and conduct ourselves accordingly?

To say that we did not "choose" to come to this country is to suggest that we need feel no obligation towards it. But that strikes me as an irresponsible attitude to take. A friend of mine maintains that she did not choose to be born and so she does not feel beholden to her parents for bringing her up. My answer to that is, "Yes, but how do your parents see it?" Even she, I am sure, would feel it somehow incumbent upon her to care for her parents in their old age. Even imperialism was not just about exploitation. For the British, there was such a thing as "the white man's burden." They left modern institutions, the rule of law and administrative practices which continue to prove their worth today.

As for having contributed to the development and prosperity of the country—the way I see it is this: the Chinese were doing it to make a living or to enrich themselves, and increasing the wealth of the country was merely a by-product of their activities. When they say that they have helped the country to grow, are they not making a virtue out of necessity? They never had it in mind to work for the good of the country, only for the good of themselves and their families. All right, so they helped to build the country, but who says they can live in it afterwards?

What is missing in our attitude, it seems to me, is any appreciation of how galling it must have been for the Malays to see us Chinese putting our stamp all over their cities, how wounded they must have been in their pride. Of course, to quote *The Malay Dilemma*, "They, more than anyone else, have been responsible for keeping this peculiar Malay problem suppressed"; it would have embarrassed them to make their feelings felt, and it is part of the Malay character "to stand aside and let someone else pass."

But this is not to say that their feelings were not intense, or that the Chinese were not insensitive to have overlooked them. Indeed, when he mentions Malay feelings in his book, Mahathir uses the words "fierce" and "explosive." And he has occasion also to refer to "*amok*," a peculiarly Malay condition which has given a new word to the English language, and which is defined in the *Concise Oxford Dictionary* as "running about in frenzied thirst for blood."

All might have seemed quiet on the surface, but underneath the apparent acceptance was a bitterness the Malays thought it impolite to express. It is unfortunate, Mahathir says, that what the Malays think of as good manners are misinterpreted by others as evidence of weakness and inferiority. As I said earlier, I consider the Malay demand for redress entirely natural and just.

Do I realise, the friend I mentioned earlier asks me, how "unusual" I am in my view that the Chinese have reason to feel grateful to Malaysia? "I don't feel grateful to any country I have lived in," she says (she has lived in China, Malaysia, England, Switzerland, Finland and Hong Kong). "I pay my taxes, I abide by the law; by working hard I contribute in my small way to the growth of the economy. Why should I have any sense of gratitude?" As a refugee from communist China she spent part of her childhood in British North Borneo, but she says she feels no gratitude to the British for having given her family shelter. Later she received a good education in England, but she was a fee paying student throughout and does not feel that anything is owed to that country.

My reply is, "When it comes to Malaysia it is not just a question of paying taxes. Your presence as an immigrant in the places you mentioned (with the exception of Malaysia) was of no account to the indigenous people—so long as you paid your taxes and abided by the law. But when you come to Malaysia, you become part of a minority which the hosts see as a threat to themselves. You are not so much checking into a hotel as moving into somebody's home. The Malays were accommodating, but what if they were vicious—where would that leave you? Perhaps you would see it my way if you had lived through *Merdeka*."

"I doubt if I would," she says, "because I would have no cause to change the way I look at life, which is that the world does not owe me a living and neither do I owe the world anything." She agrees with me on many of the points raised in this book but not on this. It is a difference not so much of opinion as of something more fundamental: of values, perhaps, or degree of commitment. I tell her that she is a rootless person who does not feel the pull of patriotism or identification with any nation.

Her approach is more utilitarian. To her, a big gap between the haves and have-nots is bad not only because it is inegalitarian but, more importantly, because it makes for an unpleasant and unstable society. If there is a gap, she feels, then something should be done about it. There should be a redistribution of the goodies and the haves should bow to that redistribution with good grace, but if they bowed to it with bad grace, that to her is unfortunate but only to be expected. If a particular Malay does me a favour, she says, then I feel grateful to that particular Malay, but not to Malays collectively.

While she believes in equalising Chinese and Malay wealth in Malaysia, she doesn't feel that anything is "owed" to the Malays by the Chinese. The difference between us, she tells me, is also one of valuation. I happen, she says, to put a high valuation on what the British and, by association, the Chinese did, which was to lay the conditions for a thriving export economy and for capitalist development and modernisation. If it hadn't been for the British and the Chinese, it would have been some other people. In the course of laying the foundations for progress, these foreigners undermined the Malay's place in society, but it was progress nevertheless. If we must speak in terms of historical right or wrong, then, from the point of view of macro-history, it was a good thing for Malaysia and, by extension, the Malays, that the British and the Chinese came.

Let me play the devil's advocate, she says. What if I were to say to the Malay, "It wasn't by your leave that we prospered." If we're supposed to feel grateful, what are we supposed to feel grateful for—for the fact that you were weak at the time of our arrival in your country? For the fact that, by being weak and powerless, you presented no competition?

Yes, I say, and also for the fact that we have continued to prosper. Unlike in the colonial days, the Malays are now in a position of power, and if we do well today under Malay rule, it is by their leave that we do so. Without Malay tolerance and goodwill, no amount of Chinese hard work, enterprise or business acumen would be enough to assure Chinese success.

But, says the devil's advocate, we pay a high price for it. For that goodwill, we accept some restraints on our economic privileges. It's an exchange, not a case of one-way Malay beneficence. My answer to that is the terms don't seem to have handicapped you unduly, to judge by your increased well-being since the Malays came to power, a well-being founded on the enormous wealth creation ushered in by Independence and the NEP.

Yet the feeling persists that the Chinese are worse rather than better off for the NEP. I shall examine this feeling in the next chapter, but to round off this one I should like to consider the premise of those who believe that the terms of Chinese incorporation into Malaysian society have become less and less equal since Mahathir came to power, and the country has become more undemocratic since the 1969 crisis. Its politics, they say, was based on power sharing between the races until that watershed year, but thereafter it degenerated to a situation where the Malays call all the shots and the other groups merely try to defend their positions.

If the other races have any influence, it is only over issues at the margins of politics, such as Chinese vernacular education or the Lion Dance at the Chinese New Year celebrations. On weightier matters, they are powerless to influence policy. This is not democratic power sharing, these observers say, decrying what they see as rising repression and declining accommodation.

There is no denying that there has been a shift since the inception of the NEP in 1971. The shift can be variously described: from *laissez-faire* to state intervention, from a mildly pro-Malay direction to a strongly pro-Malay direction and so on. When the observers I mentioned in the last paragraph describe the shift as one of rising repression and declining accommodation, their premise is that *laissez-faire* is more desirable. When they lament that the Malays are calling the shots, their premise is that the Malays should not be calling the shots. But why ever not? After all this is *Tanah Melayu*—Land of the Malays. And look at the way the Malay leadership has run the country in the decades since independence, their vision and their intellectual grasp of what needed to be done; and then consider the quality of the non-Malay community leadership. Who inspires the greater confidence?

When observers deplore the lessening of Chinese power, they are assuming that the Chinese and Malays should be equal partners to start with. But why should they make that assumption? When they remark that the Chinese are worse off politically, they mean worse off than before 1971. But why should the period before 1971 be considered the norm? After all, it was because the pre-1971 policies did not work that the 1969 riots broke out.

They say that the non-Malays are frustrated and fearful about the future. Then why has racial violence not erupted? Their answer is that it is because Malaysia still offers the Chinese opportunities for making money. Because the pie is growing, they conclude, ethnic violence is kept in abeyance.

Let me summarise these people's reasoning: Chinese and Malays should be politically equal—they were equal before 1971, now they are not, so the country is more repressive—the Chinese are repressed and frustrated—but they keep quiet because there is money to be made—so Malaysia remains ethnically stable.

Let me suggest another line of reasoning, one which does not take the political equality of the races as its premise: Malays should be dominant—they were not sufficiently dominant before 1971—so there was trouble—now they are in full control—some Chinese feel aggrieved, but many are not bothered because there is money to be made—the Malays are making money too—so the balance holds and Malaysia remains stable.

As I said, my premise is not shared by many Chinese; indeed, one Chinese I work with pronounced it "unpalatable," "contentious and hard to accept." Nor is she alone in her disgruntlement. Far from it; indeed if everybody felt the way I do, then there would have been no Chinese dilemma. But there clearly is, and, having stated my own views, it is time I stepped aside and allowed other Chinese voices to be heard.

CHAPTER 5

CHINESE GRIEVANCES

WHEREFORE Chinese grievance? A journalist for an Asian regional weekly, a long-time observer of the Malaysian scene, was recently asked whether or not the Chinese felt discriminated against in Malaysia. His answer was, "That depends on who you talk to." In the course of canvassing Chinese views on the subject of this book, this remark came back to me, for I find that what is an issue to one Chinese is not necessarily an issue to another, and if there is a Chinese dilemma, it is not one which confronts all Chinese, or at least not all Chinese equally. Whereas the Malay dilemma was generalised over the entire Malay community, the Chinese dilemma is not universal.

This is as one would expect, since no community, however small, is a monolithic block, and even a racially homogeneous community can find itself riven by divisions—of class, say, or gender or generation. My own understanding of Chinese grievances was very much helped by a written comment by a colleague of mine, a Malaysian Chinese professional woman now settled in Australia. Let me quote her: "My elder sister, born before Independence, is both sceptical and paranoiac about [Malaysian] government policies, seeing them as encroaching more and more on Chinese liberty. She is all for me to remain in Australia. Not so my younger sister, who, like me, was born after Independence. She encourages me to return to Malaysia, saying that 'Malaysia is good'."

To say that age group makes a difference to how you see Malaysia is hardly to say something new. Yet the divergence of perception between the elder and younger sisters is telling. For the elder sister, there exists a "before" and "after" (before Chinese liberty was encroached on, and after it was encroached on). Between the "before" and "after" lies the NEP, a change, to borrow some phrases from an earlier chapter, "from a gradualist, hands-off approach favouring multiracial compromise to an approach favouring far stronger state intervention and Malay-first policies." Whereas the elder sister is old enough to have been affected by that transition—and such transitions are never without cost to someone—the younger sibling came to maturity in a situation which had already gelled. After 1969, the government did take a tougher line, and those who remember a more easygoing time in the past cannot look back without feeling they have been stung.

The perceived encroachment is political as much as economic. Those who make before-and-after comparisons speak of political emasculation, pointing to the decline in the percentage of Chinese holding Cabinet positions, and to the fact that such Cabinet portfolios as are assigned to Chinese Ministers are not strategic ones. They cannot but feel that while the Chinese may react to or take issue with a policy after it has been made, as a group they have ceased to have any part in the national agenda-setting. As they see it, the MCA's role has been reduced to that of merely placating its constituency and reassuring it of the government's good intentions. The party can neither initiate nor block policies, and it can never play anything more than an ancillary role.

I think I can safely say that for the younger sister, there is no "Chinese dilemma"; she probably thinks her elder sister's paranoia misplaced. But this doesn't mean we can write it off: there is no denying the mistrust many Chinese feel. In another telling comment, my colleague explains her disquiet over my remark that the Malays are the host and what benefit we Chinese get we get on their terms, not ours. We would not want to admit this, she says, "however true it is," because of our "fear and uncertainty" that admission would invite "retribution" in the form of a further restriction of terms by the Malays. Our distrust, in other words, gets in the way of our admitting something we know to be true.

What we are saying is, "Yes, they are the indigenous people; but if we are not to lose ground to the Malays, we will have to insist on our right to live in this country." Ours is a defensive posture, adopted in the belief that our turf is threatened. You might think that the war was over, but it is not. It is as if we live essentially in reaction to the Malays.

This is one strand of the Chinese dilemma. Another is the trouble we have reconciling ourselves to our place in the Malaysian scheme of things. That place, as many see it, is subsidiary to that of the Malays. One of our ex-civil servants, now resident in Hong Kong, describes the terms of our incorporation into Malaysian society as "a franchise," the clear implication being that, unlike rights, what we have can be taken away if we don't dance to the Malay political tune.

A contemporary of mine, a Chinese born in Malaysia, will not go as far as that, but he, too, is unreconciled to the country's majority-first policy. I recently asked him if he felt he owed his primary loyalty to Malaysia. Yes, he said, but not unqualified loyalty. By this he means that only if he were considered a first-class citizen with a status and with privileges equal to those of the *Bumiputera* would Malaysia command his absolute allegiance. In other words, he does not accept that he should concede first place to the Malays. Or, to put it in another way, he does not accept the terms of his incorporation into Malaysian society, terms that were altered in 1971, he adds, without "so much as a 'by your leave'."

For many Chinese, it is not just a question of sharing the material benefits but of being recognised and accepted "as full-fledged citizens of the country." When, asks the colleague now settled in Australia, do we cease to be guests? "How long must we continue to pay the price of citizenship?"

"How long ...?" is a question which strikes many an anxious Chinese chord. It is one which bothers even those who are prepared to let bygones be bygones. Let me quote a woman who started school before Independence: "Are we to go on being grateful to [the Malays] and accept our lot indefinitely? Isn't it time for a review to ameliorate the situation for the non-Malays? Malays can still receive preferential treatment, but on a smaller scale; otherwise the scales will soon be tipped the other way as the [imbalance] is now more than redressed." A proposal for scaling back the NEP was precisely what a Chinese group named Suqiu put forward to the government in 2000. Such proposals, though, were more than could be tolerated by those Malays who staged a rally in the capital to protest what they said was a "threat" from the Chinese community. If other Chinese took Suqiu to be a test-case, they soon knew better than to question the NEP—only "extremists," they were given to understand, would step out of line in this way. Ask the government to stop favouring the Malays and you are implicitly upsetting racial harmony—that is the equation made by some sections of Malay opinion.

Rightly or wrongly, many Chinese are not reassured that the Malays will act in good faith. Can we trust them to be fair? In shifting the balance of advantage, will they know when to stop? If we lower our defences, will we find ourselves at the start of a slippery slope? If we don't complain about the NEP, will they think it is not hurting us enough and prolong it indefinitely? These are the nagging questions that the Chinese doubting Thomases have at the back of their minds.

And just as there is no homogeneity in the Chinese community, so there are moderate and extremist camps among the Malays. We may not be doing the moderates a good turn by declaring the NEP's results to be Chinese-friendly, because to do so may create openings for Malay extremists to accuse the government of being soft on the Chinese and to press it to do even more for the Malays. There is also the risk of appearing to take the Malay side—and therefore betraying our own—when we endorse the NEP. The tragedy of race is that it forces us to choose sides.

So much of what we say and do, it seems to me, stems from our fear of giving ground to the Malays and creating openings for them to weaken our position *vis-à-vis* theirs. For example, in fights over Chinese-language education (of which more later), what is at stake is not really Chinese education as such but how much ground is being "lost" to the Malays.

The distrust translates into votes for the opposition at election time. This has prompted the Malay leaders to ask despairingly, "What more do they [the Chinese] want?" "Why are they still not happy with the present government considering how well they've done under its policies?" Were it not a channel for the Chinese to vent their frustrations and grievances, the number of votes for the opposition would not have been as high.

The real-life cases of grievance I netted in my trawl through friends and acquaintances will lend some concreteness to the general remarks I have so far made. Here is one story. A Malay man has a Chinese wife. Their children are bright and, being *Bumiputera*, enjoy ample opportunities as well as state financial assistance to pursue tertiary studies. Their maternal cousins are equally bright, but have a hard time gaining places at local universities. Being of modest means, they can only study abroad with financial help, but this they have trouble getting. They naturally feel that they have been unjustly treated.

Here is another story. A bright young Chinese legal officer whose mother paid for his education by taking in washing wins a scholarship to a top American university to pursue a postgraduate degree. He applies for study leave to take up the scholarship, but while his application is strongly supported by his Malay superiors, it is ultimately turned down by over-zealous bureaucrats. By contrast, his Malay colleagues have their paths towards postgraduate studies smoothed by government encouragement and assistance. It would be unusual if this man did not feel aggrieved.

Then there is the case of the young, locally trained Chinese woman doctor. She is active in multiethnic community affairs both as a student and as a district medical officer. She is a committed contributing member of the community, sitting on various committees and working alongside community leaders. She enjoys her involvement and finds great satisfaction in her work. She passes the first part of her postgraduate exams for medicine locally. She then applies for leave to study for her Part Two exams in England, and after much to-ing and fro-ing is grudgingly given unpaid leave. Her experience is in sharp contrast to that of her Malay colleagues, whose aspirations are unequivocally and strongly supported.

There was a time when many Chinese returned from abroad fired by youthful ideals of serving Malaysia. Though there was an obvious demand for their skills, they experienced inordinate delays in getting government jobs. Those who had foreign spouses had their lives made even more difficult by the denial of residence visas to their spouses, who kept having to renew their temporary visas by shuttling to and from Singapore or Thailand. They were left with the distinct impression that they were neither wanted nor welcome in Malaysia, and who can blame them?

Then there are the thousands of Chinese teachers, police officers and other government servants who were passed over for promotion and found themselves serving under their former Malay subordinates. Lost promotions mean not only lower earnings but also diminished pensions, so that there are non-Malay retirees who feel that they are still paying for the NEP in terms of their reduced pensions. It may be a difference of only a couple of hundred dollars, but to people of limited means, that is still a lot of money.

Many small people have been hurt by Malay highhandedness and discrimination. The Chinese taxi driver may find that he is unable to get a licence of his own. The Chinese petty trader may not be allocated hawker facilities and stalls. The Chinese farmer may be evicted from "his" land. The denizen of one of the all-Chinese New Villages may see his community neglected by the government. Though only sections of the Chinese population are affected, word spreads and the sense of injury is generalised over the whole community.

What also puts Chinese backs up is the treatment they get at the hands of Malay officials when they apply for permits, licences and so on. In itself, to be cold-shouldered by officials is nothing unusual; you meet rude officials the world over. What complicates matters in Malaysia is that those cold shoulders are more often than not Malay, while the supplicants are mostly Chinese, small people working in the Chinese sector of the economy. This turns what might have been a race-neutral situation into a racially charged one. To better explain what I mean, I quote a comment by A. Kadir Jasin, the Group Editor of the *New Straits Times*, on rude and inefficient officials: "The government is paying a high price for this, and pardon me for saying that the Malays and Muslims are at risk of getting a bad name because the majority of civil servants are Malays and Muslims. I am not denying that our civil service is better in comparison with some in the neighbouring countries. Ours is more professional and efficient and less corrupt. But that is not good enough if we bear in mind that the majority of our civil servants are Muslims."

It had also annoyed some Chinese that the corporate restructuring required by the NEP entailed the allocation by most non-Malay companies of equity below market prices to Malays. But what really incensed them was that many of those who were allocated the cheap shares sold them in the open market to make a quick profit and the companies in question found they had to top up their Malay shareholdings. Others complain that all the valuable contracts and licences arising from privatisation have gone to the Malays. The many Chinese insiders and partners who shared in the gains no doubt kept quiet, but not so those who had reason to gripe. Besides, a sense of imbalance is cumulative, reinforced by such discoveries as the fact that special discounts of between 5 and 7 per cent were given to *Bumiputera* housebuyers—and unneedy ones at that.

None of this is helped when, in reply to questions in Parliament about why so many Chinese were emigrating, some Malay leaders were heard to say, "Good riddance to bad rubbish." In casting doubt on Chinese loyalty, many Malays forget that the work of the Special Branch during the Emergency was crucial to the success of the struggle against the communist insurgency, and that the Special Branch was staffed mostly by Chinese who knew that it was fellow-Chinese they were fighting. The chief of Psychological Warfare at the time, for example, was C.C. Thoo, a Chinese. Indeed if there had been as many disloyal Chinese as the Malays made out, the Emergency could not have been won.

Nor has emigration been prompted by disloyalty. Some have left for the immemorial reason, the search for a better life; others have moved to a Western country in the hope that their children's educational chances would improve thereby or because they want to be with their children who have chosen to stay on after their studies. Some emigrants simply prefer a Western lifestyle; others were prompted by their anxieties about racial strife. But the vast majority of Chinese prefer to stay in Malaysia and are at home here.

The source of Chinese disaffection may date from an earlier time but the hurt takes time to wear off. For instance, the effects of the Industrial Coordination Act of 1975, whose requirements included the putting aside of at least 30 per cent of the equity of manufacturing companies for Malays, are no longer felt by the Chinese business sector, but the resentment they provoked at the time continues to brood over many. For numerous individual Chinese, the shadow of the past bedevils the present.

What has twisted the knife has been the behaviour of the Ugly Malay, a product, it has to be said, of the NEP. One kind threatens politicians and officials, thumping tables to make *Bumiputera* claims on contracts, licences, concessions and land. Yet no sooner do they get their concessions than they sell them to the Chinese. Some even come back later to demand more money from the Chinese, threatening to denounce them as exploitative Ali Baba operators (businessmen who take on sleeping Malay partners for form's sake and because *Bumiputeras* qualify for government contracts and licences). Others got the Chinese to do the work but, instead of paying their bills to the Chinese, blew their money on conspicuous consumption.

Another kind emerges from the ranks of aspiring politicians, those who wish to be seen as being tough on the Chinese in order to gain a Malay following. Coming from the political fringes and *Bumiputera* trade groups, these specimens of the Ugly Malay use their organisational positions as a platform from which to advance their personal or political ambitions. Their conduct is offensive to Chinese and Malay alike and is a far cry from the self-effacing, diffident and polite behaviour described in *The Malay Dilemma*. The Ugly Malay gives the NEP a bad name.

Earlier in this chapter I suggested that if there was a Chinese predicament, it is the predicament of a community on the defensive. Chinese politicians are judged by how well they stand up for the residual rights of a Chinese community on the defensive. When I say "residual," I have in mind the fact that though there was a time when the Chinese believed themselves to have rights of national leadership, they have by now surrendered their claim to such leadership. Today the residual rights largely revolve around the issue of how much of their identity they must give up to become Malaysian. Since, race apart, identity is commonly defined by language, the preservation of the Chinese tongue through Chinese-language education is seen by many to be crucial to the survival of the Chinese in Malaysia as a distinct community.

Fighting to safeguard Chinese-language education is fighting for residual rights in another guise. Indeed it may be seen as the Chinese community's last stand. The right to teach and learn non-Malay languages, its champions maintain, is safeguarded by the Constitution; all is not lost, these people feel, if that right remains. It is in response to the setbacks suffered by their cause, some say, that they join the opposition.

In 1987, Chinese voices were raised to protest perceived government interference in the management of Chinese vernacular schools. In a show of Chinese solidarity, the MCA deputy president Lee Kim Sai, then Deputy Minister for Education, sat beside opposition leader Lim Kit Siang in a 2,000-strong gathering at the Tianhou Temple in Kuala Lumpur. All Chinese were asked to demonstrate their solidarity by boycotting school. In a move of "counter-solidarity," the UMNO Youth held a rally at the Merdeka Stadium. Finally, things came to a head and the government acted by arresting the combatants, both Chinese and Malay.

Many foreign observers are under the impression that the Chinese language is banned in Malaysia. This is quite mistaken. We have government-run Chinese-medium primary schools. One of the things Chinese educationists press for is more state allocation for these schools. In a book published by the MCA in 1988, the fact that Chinese primary schools accounted for 27.3 per cent of total primary school enrolment in 1984 but received only 3.4 per cent of the total government funding allocation is seen as a case of discrimination. But the reason foreign observers believe Chinese-language education to be threatened with extinction is the periodic outbreaks of Chinese anxiety over government pressure on schools to switch to Malay.

If the champions of Chinese education portray their cause as a "struggle," it is because they have taken a few hard knocks in their time. Their path, as they put it in Chinese, is *jingji zai tu*, "overgrown with brambles." Their struggle goes back to 1951, to their opposition to the colonial Barnes Education Report, which denied the need to study one's mother tongue. Then there was the post-*Merdeka* Education Act of 1961, which required all secondary schools within the national system to use either English or Malay as the medium of instruction. The bulk of the existing Chinese secondary schools fell in with the official policy, but over a dozen chose to remain autonomous and to continue to teach in Chinese. These became the first Independent Chinese Schools, which survived fitfully into the late 1960s in the face of government disapprobation.

They might have had to close their doors for lack of pupils were it not for the NEP and for the government ruling in 1971 for English primary schools to convert to Malay and for secondary schools to follow suit. The effect of this was to double the intake of the Independent Schools. The way the Chinese saw it was, since the quota system of the NEP reduced their chances of admission to tertiary educational institutions and getting jobs in the public sector anyway, there was no longer any compelling reason for them to do well in the public exams for which the national schools prepared one.

A movement for the revival of the Independent Schools was started, with hawkers, taxi-drivers, shopkeepers and barbers all donating money enthusiastically, many of them giving their days' takings. There was a heightened sense of Chinese consciousness and self-reliance. The various Chinese associations were given a new lease of life. Textbooks were revamped, buildings were erected, exams were set and conducted (recognition for which exams was won from various universities in the U.S., Britain, Canada, Australia, New Zealand and Singapore), and new leaders were thrown up. Subsequently, a proposal to establish a private multiracial and multicultural university called the Merdeka University to cater to the needs of those disadvantaged by the quota system was rejected by the government.

When you talk to champions of Chinese-language education, you cannot help but be struck by the firmness with which they hold to their cause, which they see as nothing less than the defence of "a legitimate and basic human right." To these people, what is at stake is the very survival (or submergence) of the Chinese cultural identity. In the MCA book mentioned earlier, Chua Jui Ming, currently the Minister of Health, attributes the high enrolment in mother-language primary schools to the wish of the Chinese community "to re-emphasise their own identity through their own language and culture" in the face of "a hardening Malay position in the formulation of a national culture policy based on Malay culture."

The book laments, however, that most post-*Merdeka* Chinese "do not have the depth in the Chinese language to appreciate the finer points of Chinese culture, let alone promote it. The magnitude of this phenomenon is enormous. Statistics show that almost 70 per cent of the Chinese population today belong to the post-*Merdeka* generation who are below 30 years old. The younger generation of Malaysian Chinese are not in a position to promote or sustain the same cultural heritage and values as their forefathers. This reality is indisputable. Whether by choice or circumstances, indigenous Chinese culture and values cannot be expected to grow within the Malaysian environment."

What challenges the preservation of the Chinese language is not just Malay, the national language, but also English, the international language of commerce and technology and the common language among the different racial groups. How far English gains on Chinese, or on Malay for that matter, only time will tell.

Of the top Chinese political leaders (MCA presidents), only one could be said to be Chinese-educated and even he is an English-speaker. Otherwise how could he communicate with his Malay and Indian counterparts in government? Tan Cheng Lock, the founder president of the MCA, and his son Siew Sin, also a president of the MCA, were Malaccan Babas who could not speak Chinese. Lim Kit Siang, the long-serving and combative opposition leader, is also English-educated. One of the oddities of Malaysian Chinese public life is that when political leaders wave ethnic banners and make cultural assertions, they do so in English! A friend of mine from Hong Kong tells me: "I have to laugh when I hear Lee Kuan Yew arrogating Confucianism to himself and to Singaporeans. It's hilarious, because he does it in English!" Some Chinese politicians in Malaysia produce the same comic effect.

One of the things which keeps Chinese identity strong and separate in Malaysia, ironically enough, is the continued salience of the line between *Bumiputera* and non-*Bumiputera*; were it not for the communal cast of Malaysian politics, cultural crossing would have been more intensive. Another is the sheer size of the Chinese minority. A third is the fact that the Malay-based national identity and language are yet to be fully developed. Chinese newspaper readership is expanding, a sign perhaps of a growing interest in a China that is today more open to the outside world than it has been for decades. Yet the increasing difficulty of preserving Chinese culture, in a country where there has been no fresh Chinese immigration for almost three generations, is not in any doubt.

Detribalisation is resisted by all ethnic minorities to a greater or lesser degree. Part of the Chinese dilemma in Malaysia is the fear of diminishing cultural distinctness. You feel a strong sense of transition when you turn from the hard core of the Chinese community to the young graduates of the national school system. The balance struck so far is a delicate one, and many issues relating to the identity of Malaysian Chinese remain unresolved.

To sum up then, distrust, self-defensiveness and disgruntlement are aspects of the Chinese condition in Malaysia. It is not a universal condition, nor is it always apparent to the superficial eye, but it is there beneath the surface—its causes sometimes hard to pin down exactly—like the vaguely disturbed equanimity of a person who has known bad times.

The bad times are bound up with the costs exacted by the NEP. So much Chinese disaffection is traceable to these costs that it behoves us to look at the NEP more closely. The NEP is not something that was plucked out of thin air. It was prefigured, as I have said, in *The Malay Dilemma*. But to understand the rationale behind it, we should consider the treatment of blacks by whites in America.

CHAPTER 6

THE AMERICAN DILEMMA

THE UNITED STATES is a country whose creed is: "We hold these truths to be self-evident, that all men are created equal." In theory, and according to its Constitution, it is committed to the principles of equality; in practice, wrote Gunnar Myrdal in 1944, it tolerated segregation and racial discrimination. How do you reconcile the one with the other? That, he said, was the American dilemma.

As a Swedish economist and eminent person, Myrdal had been called upon as an outsider to investigate the so-called Negro problem. The influential book he published in 1944, *An American Dilemma*, sets out his findings and views. The Negro problem, he suggested, represented the gulf between the white American ideal (of equality for all) and the reality (the denial of equality to blacks). You could not really claim America to be a land of equality when blacks had to ride at the backs of buses, use segregated bathrooms, eat in segregated restaurants, and be educated in separate (and distinctly inferior) schools because the law had decided that there was nothing unfair or unequal about separate or segregated facilities. "Separate but equal" was how the Americans described their policy towards the blacks, though you could just as easily have called it "apartheid."

I wonder if Mahathir read *An American Dilemma* before he wrote *The Malay Dilemma*, and whether the title of his book was inspired by Myrdal's? He certainly draws some parallels between the Malay situation and that of the blacks in America; "How relevant to Malaysia," he writes, "is the racial inequality in the United States? The answer, he goes on to say, is that it is "very relevant indeed." However, I should quickly point out, lest I confuse the reader, that whereas for Myrdal the plight of the blacks constituted a dilemma for the whites, for Mahathir, the Malay predicament constituted a dilemma for the Malays themselves.

I might add, while I am at it, that the two books are very different in kind: Myrdal's a scholarly tome of some 1,400 pages, addressing philosophical, moral and social issues; Mahathir's a barely 200-page long document that is polemical and clearly partisan.

I was struck by many passages in Myrdal's book. I shall quote one here, to illustrate how racist, by today's standards, even the most liberal of American liberals were in their time. Here is Thomas Jefferson, the author of the Declaration of Independence, the champion of the emancipation of slaves, and the great voice of early American liberalism, on the race problem: "Deep-rooted prejudices entertained by the whites; ten thousand recollections, by the blacks, of the injuries they have sustained; new provocations; the real distinctions which nature has made; and many other circumstances, will divide us into parties, and produce convulsions, which will probably never end but in the extermination of the one or the other race."

By "the real distinctions" between whites and blacks, he meant things like colour, hair, the black's "lack of reasoning power, lack of depth in emotion, poverty of imagination and so on." What's more, he believed that "it is not their condition, then, but nature, which has produced the distinction." For all his sympathy for the plight of the blacks, for all his censure of white prejudice, he was nevertheless prey to the racist myth of black biological inferiority.

The black rejoinder, often given with impassioned eloquence, is worth quoting; here is one by the black writer Kelly Miller (1863-1939): "The Negro has never, during the whole course of history, been surrounded by those influences which tend to strengthen and develop the mind. To expect the Negroes of Georgia to produce a great general like Napoleon when they are not even allowed to carry arms, or to deride them for not producing scholars like those of the Renaissance when a few years ago they were forbidden the use of letters, verges closely upon the outer rim of absurdity. Do you look for great Negro statesmen in states where black men are not allowed to vote?"

It is extraordinary to think that it was only as late as 1954 that American blacks acquired the genuine legal substance of equality. That was the year a Supreme Court decision in *Brown v. Board of Education of Topeka* opened the doors of an all-white school to a little black girl called Linda Brown, and thereby put an end to the "separate but equal" policy. Yet a judicial ruling was one thing, human behaviour quite another. The law might forbid it, but bus drivers still ordered black passengers to sit at the back. Making the majority live up to the letter of its own laws took a ten-year civil rights struggle on the part of the minority. It was not until 1964 that a Civil Rights Act outlawing segregation in all public facilities was signed into law.

All this happened decades after Myrdal pointed out the unpalatable contradiction at the heart of America. He might never have written his book, for all the effect that it had on public policy at the time. Yet what he proposed was clear enough. Race relations improved or deteriorated, he suggested, on a cumulative principle. Consider a people who are poor, dirty and inept because they have been discriminated against. Because they appear poor, dirty and inept, they will suffer still more discrimination. And so it goes on, in a vicious cumulative circle.

But suppose a few individuals in their group were shown to be rich, clean and accomplished. Then not only will these individuals not be discriminated against because they appear rich, clean and accomplished, but their success will reflect on their own people, and the entire people may suffer less discrimination because they cannot now be dismissed wholesale as hopeless beyond redemption. What is more, the few individuals may inspire others in their group to emulate them and become rich, clean and accomplished too. Their people will take pride in the prestige of these individuals, and hold up their own heads instead of being sunk in apathy, and in doing so they will themselves better their chances of succeeding. Eventually the whole process becomes self-sustaining, and the vicious cumulative circle is broken and becomes a virtuous one.

The logic behind this might be called the logic of "role models." To create these models, it is necessary to give them extra help—in other words, to practise what came to be called positive discrimination or affirmative action. The NEP is affirmative action by another name.

"Role model" is now a part of everyday American vocabulary. Mahathir does not use the term, but it is what he has in mind when he defends the appointment of token Malay directors in large non-Malay companies. Such appointments were made to meet the government's positive discrimination requirements. Everyone knows, he says, that these Malays are merely selling their names and cashing in on the government's policies. Everyone knows that they are not "true" directors. But then you have to start somewhere. How else, other than by admitting a few Malays into the boardroom, are you going to wean people from the idea that Malays can never sit on boards of directors? Their mere presence, Mahathir suggests, is a breach in the walls of non-Malay bias and prejudice.

It may seem to many poor Malays grossly unfair, he says, that these directors have grown rich not through their own ability or effort, but through privilege and government favour. But, he counters, and I quote: "if these few Malays are not enriched the poor Malays will not gain either. It is the Chinese who will continue to live in huge houses and regard the Malays as only fit to drive their cars. With the existence of the few rich Malays at least the poor Malays can say that their fate is not entirely to serve the rich non-Malays. From the point of view of racial ego, and this ego is still strong, the unseemly existence of Malay tycoons is essential."

To put it in another way, Malay tycoons are essential as role models. If you only ever see Malays as drivers of Chinese cars, you will never think of them as anything other than drivers. And even the Malays will believe this, and will live up (or perhaps "down" is the better word) to their own poor self-perception. But show them a few Malay tycoons and their dignity as Malays (their "racial ego," as Mahathir calls it) will be restored. And surely it is much easier to succeed when you are racially confident than when you are not? Like Myrdal, Mahathir is arguing for the start of a virtuous cumulative circle through government intervention.

Racial peace will only prevail, he says, when there is racial equality. Few people will disagree with this viewpoint. But not everyone has the same conception of racial equality. For some people, racial equality can be said to exist only when everyone is treated alike, regardless of racial category. So to treat Malays as special is to discriminate racially and to practise racial inequality. By extension, Malaysia is seen by these people as a racially unjust country. Their catchphrases are "equal rights" and "equality of opportunity."

For others such as Mahathir, however, racial equality means something different: it is a state of affairs in which the races are roughly equal on all important measures. In the case of Malaysia, it can only be said to exist when the average income of the Malays, say, is as high as that of the Chinese. It is a sort of statistical equality, an equality of results rather than equality of rights or opportunity.

How to achieve racial equality, however conceived, is also matter for disagreement. Allocation in society is normally made through market mechanisms or through bureaucratic systems operating according to the rules of formal justice. But if it is shown that under such systems one race does consistently less well than another, then some people believe that there should be a bending of the rules through affirmative action to achieve percentage parity between the two. Others are completely opposed to this kind of intervention, seeing it as an interference with the market and with the system of formal justice.

Then there is a third group, whose position is betwixt and between. Affirmative action can take a number of forms. It can mean monitoring the proportions of a less successful race in a particular profession and offering the training necessary for a percentage, equal to that of the more successful race, to be attained. But it can also mean promoting the incompetent so as to fill the quota of positions set aside for members of the less successful race.

The members of the third group are not against affirmative action as such, but they are strongly opposed to racially based quotas. Interestingly enough, many successful middle-class blacks in America fall into this category. Some of them have written books on the subject, and as their arguments bear on Malaysia's NEP, I will take a closer look at what they say in the next chapter.

CHAPTER 7

AFFIRMATIVE ACTION: AMERICAN AND MALAYSIAN EXPERIENCES

WHAT have successful, middle-class American blacks got against affirmative action? About half a dozen things. Let me consider them one by one (though not in any order of importance) and see whether they apply in any way to how the NEP has worked out in Malaysia.

First, these critics say that one of the worst effects of affirmative action is a kind of demoralisation. It increases rather than mitigates the black's personal self-doubt. The message it sends to its beneficiaries is: "You are backward." Because of affirmative action, its critics say, blacks can never feel certain that they are as good as any white they work with, and know that many whites are certain that they are not. A white sees a black in a prestigious job and, consciously or unconsciously, thinks he is in that job because normal standards have been lowered to increase black representation. And even if a black knows that he is competent in his own right, he knows that whites do not, so that, consciously or unconsciously, he still feels inferior. Because of that feeling of inadequacy, the feeling that affirmative action is doing for him what he cannot do for himself, his ability to perform is undermined and he ends up confirming the whites in their belief that he is unfit for the job.

But this is not the case in Malaysia. In fact, today the Malays are probably more at ease with themselves than they had been for a very long time. In 1970 Mahathir wrote in *The Malay Dilemma*, "They are not proud of the 'privilege' of being protected by law like cripples. They would like to get rid of these privileges if they can, but they have to let pride take second place to the facts of life." Far from damaging that pride, affirmative action has restored it to them, and nowadays you can't be in Malaysia long and not feel the confidence of the new generation of Malays. The NEP has bred self-worth rather than self-doubt.

A passage I came across in a 1993 book by the Malaysian journalist Rehman Rashid, called *A Malaysian Journey*, illustrates how confident and secure the new breed of Malays are. The author is talking to three twenty-year-olds. Their fathers are Malay, their mothers not. At one point he mentions the NEP. To his astonishment one of the three young Malaysians asks him, "What's the NEP?" The author is incredulous, but he finds that they are not joking; these youngsters whom he calls the true children of the NEP really don't know what the initials stand for.

He contrasts this telling conversation with one he had with a group of eighteen-year-olds some years earlier. He asked the two Malay boys in the group if they could survive without the NEP. They both shook their heads. And when he asked them why not, they couldn't give him an answer. The NEP was like "the crutches that help an injured person walk again," he told them, "or like the scaffolding for a new building .... Once the building is finished, the scaffolding comes down." The NEP will "only have succeeded when no one thinks about it, or talks about it, or believes they need it any more." He asked the two Malay boys if the day might come when they would no longer remember the NEP, or feel it, or know it. Again they shook their heads and said, "No."

But here he is, only a few years later, chatting with Malaysians who neither feel it nor remember it, who, indeed, have never even heard of the NEP. He marvels at these new Malaysians, at how free they are of the burden of expectations "imposed upon the Malays in the effort to exorcise their insecurities." These people are anything but debilitated by uncertainty.

And they are but three of many. Today young Malays find role models everywhere, in the boardroom, in the professions, in the universities, in the executive suites of corporate Malaysia, each of them the very image of the aspirant achiever. They are all testimony to the fact that the Malay population has entered a virtuous circle, as greater prosperity produces greater self-confidence and greater self-confidence in turn leads to greater prosperity.

Of course, the corruption in preferential treatment is the hidden incentive to be dependent on the government. A second complaint made by its critics in America is that there is a dilemma at the heart of affirmative action: it is supposed to be a spur, but it actually rewards its beneficiaries for falling behind. In helping people, there is always the danger of making them less self-reliant.

That danger has not escaped right-thinking Malays. They are keenly aware of it, and what is more they want to do something about it. At the UMNO Youth General Assembly in November 1993, for example, one of the resolutions adopted called for the replacement of the educational subsidy for Malay students with an incentive scheme, doing away with the "dependence syndrome" and creating a competitive society. These are encouraging signs, though it remains to be seen how quickly words will translate into action.

A third complaint black Americans make against affirmative action is that it encourages its beneficiaries to exploit their own past victimisation as a reason for present privilege. Racial preference comes to be seen as reparation for historical wrongs. The temptation is to play on white guilt, to believe, "The whites owe it to us." To justify preference, the blacks must constantly portray whites as oppressors and themselves as victims. In this way they come to have a vested interest in the victim role, and to end up as excuse-seekers rather than strivers.

It is certainly tempting to blame the Chinese for the plight of the Malays in the years before the inception of the NEP. It is tempting for Malays to say, "We were doing very nicely until the massive immigration of the Chinese into our country." In his book Mahathir speaks of a Malay retreat before a Chinese onslaught, and describes how, with the huge wave of Chinese immigrants, the Malays found themselves displaced in petty trading and all sectors of skilled work. Whatever the Malays could do, Mahathir says, the Chinese could do better and more cheaply. As a result, the Malays were completely edged out of the economic action.

Yet this is a charge that is not laid against the Chinese today. To be fair, Mahathir says in his book, the Malays themselves must shoulder some of the blame for their economic backwardness. His book sees the Chinese as part of the problem rather than the whole problem. That the need for affirmative action is all the fault of the Chinese is a seductive idea, but it is one to which the Malays don't succumb. As Anwar Ibrahim, the one-time deputy prime minister, put it, their growing self-assurance means that "they will not use the Chinese as a scapegoat for their own failure."

What else is wrong with affirmative action? The whole idea of proportionate representation (or quotas), its American critics say. This is the idea that races must be represented according to their proportion in society. (And not just races but also sexes: feminists demand numerical targets based on gender.) Because underrepresentation by blacks (or women) in good jobs is taken as a proof of racial discrimination (or sexism), employers simply fill the appropriate number of slots with blacks (or women) in order to pre-empt accusations of racism (or sexism).

Likewise at universities. Filling a set number of places with black students gives the appearance of racial fairness, but it is mere window-dressing, the critics say, because six years later only a little over a quarter of these students will actually graduate. The higher rate of admission masks the high rate of failure. "Proportionate representation" encourages people to think that all you have to do is to change the numbers and the races are in balance.

Statistical representation is not without its risks in Malaysia either. There is, for example, the risk of intellectual mediocrity. There is the risk of faked transfer of Chinese-owned shares to Malay companies. There is the risk of so-called Ali Baba businesses. Yet no one can deny that taken as a whole, the Malays have been truly and not just cosmetically uplifted.

To discriminate positively in favour of any group of people is to widen their opportunities. Many problems still can stand in the way of these people making the best use of the enlarged opportunities. Malays have far fewer of these problems than black Americans, whose lesser start in life is often rooted in stumbling blocks like family breakdown and growing up in unstable homes in city slums. Setting quotas by race doesn't really get to the heart of the matter in America.

Many Malays are well aware that they are not necessarily doing themselves a good turn by having their path smoothed for them. Earlier I mentioned the call by the UMNO Youth General Assembly for real competition in the field of education. Some want the establishment of first-rate educational institutions where merit, not race, is the basis for admission, no doubt because they feel they can hold their own in any competition. They feel they can best any rival. And if this is not an indication that real, rather than merely apparent, educational advance has been achieved by the Malays, then it is hard to know what is.

The fifth objection raised at affirmative action is that it polarises race relations. It sets one race against another. This is not to say that they were not pitted against each other in the first place; Chinese and Malays were set at loggerheads during and after the Japanese Occupation, the reader may remember from an earlier chapter. But the critics of affirmative action argue that its effect is to make racial friction inevitable. Every advantage gained by one race only calls the other to arms.

Has this been the NEP's effect in Malaysia? The fundamental question in politics is: who, in a given population, is considered "us" and who is considered to be "them"? I am afraid that the NEP has had the effect of strengthening the sense of "us" and "them" between the Malays and the Chinese. I think that Malay politicians must accept some of the responsibility for having encouraged the view among the Malays that the Chinese are a threat. Being seen as a threat, as "them," heightens the Chinese sense of "us." Perhaps the Chinese would not have insisted so much on their "rights" if these rights weren't seen to be something that "they" were taking away from "us." The NEP, of course, has been seen as the instrument by which their rights were downgraded to second class.

Similarly, the importance of "Chinese culture" gets inflated by its correlation with issues of political and economic equity. The Chinese have become more defensive, and feel that it would not do to give in because if they conceded an inch, the Malays would take an all. Feeling their position under threat, they assert their "culture" the more. So the heightened assertion of Chineseness does seem to be a fallout of affirmative action.

I have left to last the most controversial objection to affirmative action. This is the contention that it has failed to help the most needy members of the target group, and that this failure can be seen in every country where it has been practised, Malaysia included. True, sceptics say, it may help the target group to do better, but the benefits flow disproportionately to the better off or most fortunate members of that group, the very people who need it the least.

Of these sceptics, perhaps no one is more influential than the black American scholar Thomas Sowell, whose lack of confidence that affirmative action will actually work makes itself felt on every other page of his book, *Preferential Policies: An International Perspective*. His survey, which covers India, Nigeria, Sri Lanka, the United States and Malaysia, produces a balance sheet of the most dismal and pessimistic kind.

I am not competent to judge his treatment of the other countries, but I am not persuaded that he has the last word on the NEP. Of course, he wrote his book some years ago and things have changed a great deal since 1984, the last date for which he had data. I am sure that if he were to update his book, he would have to modify his pessimism about the impact of the NEP. It is hard to say at what point the policy began to bite, but my impression is that Sowell wrote his book before its effects became clearly visible.

Furthermore, I thought as I read his book, there is something wrong with the way he argues his case and draws his conclusions. For example, he takes the decline of the number of non-Malays in the police and armed forces as a sign that the non-Malays have lost out under the NEP. He has clearly neglected to factor into his equation the traditional Chinese disdain for soldiering—as the saying goes, "Just as good iron is not wrought into nails, so good men do not become soldiers." It is a well-known fact that the Chinese don't sign up during the forces' recruitment campaigns.

As for his conclusion that affirmative action invariably fails to deliver on its promise, you've only got to look around you to see that he is being over-hasty—after all, you can't miss the evidence of Malay upward mobility. There must be any number of middle-class Malays who started life as poor *kampung* kids, and who are now well-to-do urban professionals, thanks to the NEP. But I know that by itself anecdotal evidence is not enough to persuade people to switch their opinion, so I have decided to present my counter-argument in the form of statistics too.

His basic argument is that the ends don't justify the means. Intention is one thing, he suggests, consequences are quite another. Yet the intention of the NEP was the redistribution of the country's wealth, and it is common knowledge that by 1990, the Malay share of the national corporate cake was only a little short of the 30 per cent aimed for by the NEP—and this was from a starting point of as little as 2 per cent. Of course, this is not to say that the Malays have acquired a corresponding share of the national economy but it does say that in this case, contrary to Sowell, consequence does match intention.

Another goal was to better the lot of the people at the bottom of the economic heap regardless of racial category. Again, aim and result tally. In the fourteen years between 1973 and 1987, the proportion of Malaysians falling into the "Poor" category almost halved. The middle class as a whole grew nearly one and a half times larger, but the number of middle-class Malays rose by a steep 76 per cent, as against a 19 per cent increase for Chinese and a 31 per cent increase for Indians.

There are other yardsticks of success. Take occupation. Malays have made huge inroads into the professions. In 1970, only one out of every ten doctors in Malaysia was Malay. By 1990, that rate had nearly tripled. During the same period, the proportion of Malay architects more than doubled, as did that of Malay dentists, while that of Malay engineers went up from about 19 per cent to about 35, and that of lawyers from about 15 per cent to 22. I don't think I need say anything about these figures: that they indicate impressive strides is self-evident.

That said, it must be admitted that the NEP's benefits have not fallen on all classes of Malays equally. To be fair to Sowell, he does have a point when he says that the chief Malay gainers from the NEP have been those at the top of the Malay economic heap. The Malaysian study he cites—

showing that while the number of Malays on corporate boards of directors rose under the NEP, so did the proportion of Malays among the population living below the poverty line—is now a bit of out of date, but it is true that the bottom 40 per cent of Malay households got a smaller share of the total income of the Malay population in 1984 than in 1973. By 1987, the share has grown bigger, but by only a tiny amount, it has to be said.

Between 1973 and 1987, the largest gain was in the proportion of Malays classed as "Rich": this went up no less than fivefold, a huge rise by any standard (the corresponding rate for Chinese was two and a half). The proportion of Malays classed as "Poor" was halved during that period, but, interestingly enough, that of Chinese shrank to less than a quarter of what it was in 1973. To go by these figures, then, the NEP would seem to have done more to better the lot of the Chinese poor than that of their Malay counterparts. Relatively speaking, it emerges, the rich Malays and the poor Chinese made the biggest headway.

The NEP has its snags—which policy hasn't? I am not able to defend it against every one of the criticisms that have been levelled against preferential policies, but I think I am justified in giving it a score of four out of six, which is a pretty good number. Just as a medicine is judged by its efficacy, so a policy is evaluated by asking how far it delivers on its promise—has it done what it purports or is supposed to do? Broadly speaking that has been Sowell's approach. But it is only one way of appraising the NEP.

To explain what I mean, let me use the medicine analogy again. No medicine is without its adverse effects. Yet that doesn't stop us from taking medicines. Why? Because we reckon we will feel still worse without them. For all its shortcomings, there is no question that we are still better off with the NEP than without. To realise the truth of this, you have only to ask yourself the question: "What if there were no NEP?"

To me the answer is obvious. There would have been a disaster scenario. There would have been an enormously widened gulf between Malays and non-Malays, and there would have been a dangerously lopsided economy, inviting Malay despair, disaffection, hatred and violence. All this weighing of who gains and who loses obscures a fundamental fact: that if the Malays lose, then the Chinese lose too; because if racial hatreds tore the country apart, then everyone loses.

But, I hear dissenters say, granted that the imbalance has to be corrected, is the NEP the best way to do it? Why can't we, in other words, get to the same place by a different route? This is the plea of many Malaysian Chinese. But if not the NEP, then what? Some black American intellectuals believe that there is a middle way, a colour-blind way. Help a man because he is poor, they say, not because he is black.

I hear a familiar ring to their argument: it is the same as saying underprivilege is a matter of class, not race. Myself, I am a realist, and I don't think race is something you can wish away. Besides, it is unfortunately the case that class and race lines often coincide. If anybody can come up with a better way of righting the imbalance that existed in Malaysia in 1970, I would like to hear it. Besides, affirmative action was already built into the Constitution. Turn the clock back to 1957, the time of Independence, and see if any other means were available. The answer has to be No.

CHAPTER 8

CRITICISMS OF AFFIRMATIVE ACTION

IT MAY BE WONDERED why I keep bringing the American race problem into the picture. What has the U.S. got to do with the Chinese dilemma? The answer is, a great deal. How the Chinese view their lot in Malaysia can't help but be influenced by international opinion, mediated through the Western press or more direct forms of communication, and the prime shaper of that opinion, for good or ill, is America.

The ripples of public debate in America, on race as on much else, spread far and wide beyond its national borders. The world's perception of the NEP is coloured by the current backlash against affirmative action, and if foreign observers sniff at the NEP, it is partly because so many Americans, blacks included, deplore affirmative action as practised in their country. Affirmative action gets a bad press these days, and the NEP is tarred with the same brush. This is why, in the previous chapter, I made a point of spelling out the ways in which affirmative action is different, or has worked differently, in Malaysia.

Americans feel frustrated with affirmative action because it doesn't seem to have worked. But there is more to the American disenchantment than mere frustration. There is resentment. There is resentment at the individual level: you resent the fact that the preferential hiring of another race lessens your chance of getting hired yourself. But there is also resentment at a general level: you resent preferential treatment on principle because it clashes so profoundly with American ideals of fairness and equality. It is a profoundly American belief that effort is individual, and that it is according to their own efforts that individuals should be rewarded. The idea of group rights contradicts this belief. I think both kinds of resentment are felt in the Malaysian Chinese community, though, not being American, it probably feels the second kind less keenly.

As I have noted in an earlier chapter, equality means different things to different people. I know I'm generalising, but I think that, given the nature of their values, it is true to say that the notion of "equality of results" (rather than "of opportunity") strikes an unsympathetic chord in the American breast. To many Americans, adopting measures to ensure a predetermined result, even if that result is a more level playing field, is like rigging the vote or the market. Fair competition, open standards, playing by the rules—all these are American enthusiasms, and commendably so. Yet if you look for institutionalised unfairness or rule-breaking in the American political system, you will find it there too. Just think of manipulations like gerrymandering, where voters are divided into electoral districts in such a way as to give undue influence to some party or group. Think of the use of the filibuster, in which the will of the majority may be thwarted by the minority taking advantage of the rule of unlimited debate in the Senate to talk a Bill to death). Hardly democratic, these practices nonetheless exist.

Any talk of ends justifying means triggers an antipathetic reflex in them—it's what communists say of their methods, after all. And any mention of the Chinese having only second-class rights in Malaysia instantly brings out the human rights champion in the American. Yet, at the same time, many Americans would probably agree with Mahathir that it's no good saying to a black, "Come and get it, it's all yours if you're prepared to do as we do." They know what would happen if there were an unfettered play of market forces, a free-for-all. They know this, but the belief in "the survival of the fittest" is so natural to them that they can't bring themselves to endorse a policy that goes exactly against it. Yet there is the existence of antitrust legislation in the U.S. to guard against controlling monopolies, and what is affirmative action if not the attempted cartel-busting of the dominant group? Affirmative action is to make the chances more equal, just like the handicap imposed on the superior competitor in golf or the divisions applied in league football. And beyond any conception of justice, there is the Christian notion of charity, even duty, whose manifestation is everywhere evident in the West in the form of help for the disadvantaged.

Though some critics come right out and say that affirmative action is unfair, many more justify their distaste by falling back on the argument that it doesn't work, so why not abandon it; or else by claiming that they are not against affirmative action as such, only against quotas, as if the two things were separable.

It's fair yet not fair: that is how many people view preferential treatment. I see it as a paradox at the heart of the race question in America. It has echoes in the Chinese community in Malaysia, which is also torn between one version of fairness and the other. I am sure many Chinese will agree that it is only fair to divide the economic pie up more evenly, yet at the same time Malay privileges strike them as unfair.

Two things compound their dilemma. One is their belief that Malay advance is at their expense. Many Chinese still believe that economics is a zero-sum game. They think that if others have too many dumplings, they will end up with just the bowl. The second is a feeling of political impotence. The Malays have political might on their side, quite apart from the fact that they are the majority and can win by force of numbers. Fears were expressed by the Chinese in the 1980s that the Malays would unilaterally restructure the economy to the detriment of the non-Malays.

This is what foreign observers have in mind when they describe Malaysia as a racist country. By definition affirmative action is an anti-racist measure, but apparently not when it favours a majority backed by state power. They see the Malays as holding all the cards—so what is to stop them from grabbing everything for themselves?—and they cast the Chinese in the role of the victim and underdog.

Yet I would ask them to look at the situation through Malay eyes. Here is what Mahathir said in an interview in 1979: "We are the Negroes in this country .... Here the blacks are in charge. What is a fact is that because of their struggle the blacks in America are able to get to places they never got to before. This is what we are trying to do here—not by taking what belongs to others, but by securing a place for us here. No other country has tried this kind of experiment. We are doing it very nicely, very slowly. I am not anti-Chinese in any way, but I feel Malays must have a place in the sun, otherwise there is going to be bitterness, which is no good for anybody."

It will be no good for anybody whichever side of the racial divide bitterness is engendered, Malay or Chinese. The Malays can no more have things all their own way than the Chinese can, if they are not to kindle Chinese bitterness. The Malaysian government is committed to a pro-Malay policy, but it is also sticking with free market economics. The two don't always mesh, and the trick is to pursue both without causing a clash. That takes political adroitness, a quality which the government has displayed in abundance. When, with the slump in the mid-1980s, it saw a need to temper its restrictions on foreign ownership, it quietly and pragmatically did. Afterwards the economy grew at a healthy clip, and for defusing racial tension, an expanding cake which is seen to be divided up reasonably equitably is hard to beat.

Ironically, a case can be made for seeing the congruence of preferred race with state power as a good thing. Because Malays control the machinery of state, they are better able to ensure that the NEP works smoothly. I realise that, to some people, this spells a hegemony of the Malay majority and cannot conceivably be a good thing. But I don't mean it is a good thing in every instance, only in the case of Malaysia, where the government has acted with restraint and tolerance.

I doubt if positive discrimination policies in favour of Malays would have worked as well if they had been overseen by non-Malays. If blacks were running the government in America instead of whites, I'm sure affirmative action would have worked out differently there too. Imagine putting a poacher in charge of an estate instead of a gamekeeper and you will see what I mean. It is only too easy to do things half-heartedly if you are dictating and controlling the preferential treatment of a people not your own, and it may be that, in an undertaking as ambitious and as complex as this, doing things by halves is worse than doing nothing.

Many Chinese, I know, would have been happier with half measures. Special Malay privileges are nothing new: they hark back to the British colonial days. But those privileges lacked the comprehensiveness of the NEP and the Chinese thought they could live with them. It was the thoroughness with which the NEP was pursued that they found hard to take. Many felt bruised by it. Finding academic avenues closed to them, a large number chose to emigrate, to Australia, Canada and Britain.

Yet despite the NEP, or because of it, many Chinese have become rich beyond their wildest dreams. Yet these are some of the people who complain the loudest about discrimination. It is hard to convince the non-Malays (and I include the Indians in this designation) that in their case the NEP has not disadvantaged them. If you point out to a non-Malay top civil servant that he has done very well for himself he will say, "Ah, but I would have done even better if I were Malay." I once suggested to a non-Malay chief executive of a bank that his being Indian hadn't prevented him from reaching the top, and his answer was: "You know what I'd be doing if I were Malay? I'd be heading a bigger bank."

Do these people sincerely believe that they have been discriminated against on account of race? Or are they just saying so? I have earlier described some who have grounds for feeling genuinely disgruntled. Others find it convenient to blame discrimination rather than their own inadequacies when their achievement falls short of their aspirations. Still others are unsure, but are happy enough to fall in with the prevailing view. It is as tempting to plead an unfair disadvantage when you lose as it is to claim a victory against all the odds when you win.

Besides, disadvantage cuts both ways: it can deter you or it can spur you to greater effort. The Japanese, for example, are forever saying that it was their lack of natural resources which raised them to their heights of endeavour. I have already mentioned the Jews, a people honed rather than hindered by persecution. I have also quoted Burke, who said that "Our antagonist is our helper." Cosseting has its dangers. Mahathir was well aware of this when he said in *The Malay Dilemma* that denying Malays special protection would toughen them and make them competitive against all comers. "Unfortunately," he added, "we do not have four thousand years to play around with."

This brings me to my final comment on the criticisms of affirmative action. It is said, notably by Sowell, that preferential policies are always extended beyond their originally stated spans. Sowell is right on this score. The temporary does have an awkward habit of becoming permanent; the NEP has been succeeded by the National Development Policy (NDP). But my point is that the time horizon should have been longer in the first place. Twenty years, the NEP was supposed to last, and its aim was no less than the restructuring of a whole society! Had they been more experienced, the NEP's architects would not have given it so short a life. Four thousand years, Mahathir said. Exaggerated as that figure is, he is right to imply that changing the habits and attitudes of a people takes generations. So it is all the more remarkable that the NEP has brought forth a self-assured, competitive Malay bourgeoisie only twenty years down the road.

Just one final word: here I am gamely defending the NEP on paper, but if I were a big company or powerful industry, I'd be hiring publicists and PR consultants to do it for me. If the average consumer is nervous about eating genetically modified food, for instance, the biotech industry launches a million-dollar campaign to convince him that he has nothing to fear. And no eyebrows are raised at this. We all know that smoking damages health, so why is every little concession made to this fact by the powerful tobacco industry such a hard-won battle? A society in which it is the gun industry and its lobbyists, rather than the victims of violence, who determine the laws governing the availability of firearms is, thankfully, still foreign to us Asians. What defies reason is why so immoral a lobby can enjoy complete legitimacy when the Malaysian government's protection of Malays in the interest of equality and social stability is routinely greeted with head-shaking.

CHAPTER 9

IMMIGRANT CHINESE SOCIETY

IN HIS BOOK, Mahathir says that life in China through the centuries is a litany of natural and man-made disasters and this, in the course of evolution, has produced a hardy and resourceful people. By contrast, heredity and environment have combined to debilitate the Malays. He goes on to identify those traits of Malay character which, he reckons, will have to be changed before Malays can become more competitive commercially. His chief concern being the condition of the Malays, he does not go into Chinese culture or characteristics except to note some of the Chinese community's exclusive business ties and practices. Such characteristics, on the other hand, are very much part of the concern of my little book.

To talk nowadays of national character is to invite accusations of racism. The accusations are sometimes justified, but quite often not. They are frequently knee-jerk reactions to things which have not been thought through. For example, *The Malay Dilemma* was deemed racist because it invokes heredity to account for differences between the Chinese and the Malays. It is not done these days to impute common characteristics to people on the basis of race because of what happened to Jews in Nazi Germany. Yet all Mahathir is really saying is that the Malays and the Chinese are what they are because of their historical experiences; he is not proposing anything as baleful as the notion, utterly discredited by right-thinking people these days, that race determines behaviour.

Nor is it done these days to stereotype people, I am told. When Mahathir says that the Malay is fatalistic and self-effacing, and the Chinese shrewd and thrifty, he is said to be stereotyping them, and stereotyping is considered racist. Of course it is racist to think that all Chinese are shrewd and therefore they must all be prevented from becoming shopkeepers, or that all Malays are fatalistic and so nothing need be done for any one of them. Yet the fact remains that many Chinese are shrewd and a large number of Malays are fatalistic. The awkward thing about stereotypes is that there is some truth to them.

I shall no doubt be accused of stereotyping, if not racism, for what I am about to say of the Chinese. In my own defence I should like to offer this story. A Chinese immigrant arrives in England for the first time and asks a newsagent for the paper that most people buy. He is handed a copy of the *Sun*. This paper is an example of tabloid journalism of the worst possible kind. He can't believe his eyes, and asks the newsagent for the country's second favourite paper. The newsagent gives him the *Daily Mirror*, which is little better. He goes away thinking, "Popular taste in this country is low indeed."

But wait a minute, an Englishman will protest. You haven't read the *Times* and the *Guardian*. You mustn't think all Englishmen are as you think. You won't get a feel for the real

England if you go by just the *Sun* and the *Daily Mirror*. The Englishman is right, of course. Our Chinese immigrant's image of his host country is over-simplified. Nevertheless, a very large proportion of the British population accords with the Chinese immigrant's image of the nation.

Similarly, however simplified they may seem to some, my remarks will ring a few bells, I'm sure, among many Malaysian Chinese.

Notice that I write "Malaysian Chinese." I don't always use the qualifying prefix, but that is for the sake of convenience, not because I presume to speak for all Chinese, though quite often Malaysian Chinese characteristics will be observed in other Southeast Asian Chinese as well. Every Chinese has his own view of what is or is not Chinese, just as not all Australians, say, are agreed on what is typically Australian and what is not. It is a fact, though, that the imputation of negative qualities to a group will result in more disagreement among its members than the imputation of positive ones. For example, if a Chinese says, "we are a hardworking race," all Chinese heads, I expect, will nod vigorously. But if he says, "Never trust a Chinese," he will find his remark disputed by many of his countrymen.

When a Malaysian Chinese tells you the Chinese are typically this or that, or they are such and such by nature, his views will not coincide with those of the Beijing Chinese. This is natural enough, since the sample on which he bases his perception is different from that on which the Beijing Chinese bases his. The Malaysian Chinese may think he is describing Chinese in general, but he is really only describing one or two particular kinds of Chinese.

What kinds of Chinese? First, they are Chinese who live outside China. Often, in invoking what to him are typically Chinese qualities, a Malaysian Chinese is really invoking a mix of Chinese and immigrant qualities. It has often been observed that the Chinese overseas are more successful than their cousins at home. But then so are the Indians overseas, the Lebanese overseas, the expatriate Scots, the Irish Americans, and so on. Emigration sorts out those with the get-up-and-go spirit from those without. There is something called the "immigrant drive" which propels you forward and upward, and immigrants are typically upwardly mobile.

Being an immigrant is all about raising yourself by your own bootstraps, working hard for what you want, making your fortune, being resourceful, enterprising and adaptable and, above all, struggling and surviving. This is why it has been observed all over the world that, after a period, the average income of immigrants invariably outstrips that of the natives. It is no wonder, then, that the Malays found themselves outpaced by the Chinese economically. They were competing against people who had not just one but two comparative advantages: they were Chinese, and they were immigrants. To attribute immigrant Chinese competitiveness to historical circumstances in China itself is to tell only part of the story.

What other kind of Chinese is he describing when the Malaysian Chinese enlarges upon "the typical Chinese?" The kind from the southern coast of China. The southern coastal Chinese is a regional variant, not representative of the whole, but because his is the kind you see all over Southeast Asia, you are misled into believing that all Chinese are like him. With the land mass to one side of him but the sea to the other, the southern coastal Chinese is less earthbound, less inward looking than his countrymen in the interior of China.

Those who originate in southern Fujian (the ancestral home of the Hokkien speakers in Malaysia) look back to a tradition of seafaring and overseas trading. Similarly, those hailing from Guangdong (the ancestral home of Cantonese, Teochiu and most Hakka speakers) are descended from forbears who were among the first Chinese to come into contact with the West, Canton being the only port in China to be opened consistently to European trade.

People are moulded by their history, and a potent contributor to the Malaysian Chinese character is the historical legacy of coastal and overseas contact and trade. You often hear it said that the Chinese are instinctive entrepreneurs. People who say this go by their own experience, yet it is experience based on a limited sample of Chinese: the ones encountered in Hong Kong, say, or Taiwan or Malaysia, all places with immigrant Chinese populations of predominantly southern coastal origins.

To recapitulate, then, immigration and regional origin make for a difference in Chinese character. There is a third factor, which I shall call social class for want of a better term. In classical times, the ideal arrangement of Chinese society was a ladder in which the top rung was occupied by the so-called scholar-officials, the second by peasants, the third by artisans, and the fourth and last by merchants. In that scheme, merchants (in other words, traders and shopkeepers) were the lowest of the low. In practice, this ceased to be the case roughly halfway through China's recorded history. Wealth bought its possessors social mobility, and merchants rose to the second rung of the ladder, relegating the peasants to the bottom. The scholars, however, remained topdogs.

In Malaya and all other overseas Chinese communities, this classification did not obtain. How could it? You did not emigrate if you were a scholar-official. You emigrated because you wanted to make your fortune or to seek a way out of your penury. You went in search of opportunities, and such opportunities came in one of two forms: in the form of labouring jobs, or in the form of commerce. Those who lived by the first could be classed as artisans, and by the second, as merchants. So in terms of the traditional Chinese ladder, there were really only two rungs in Malaya. There was no peasantry, and though there were some pen-pushers, bookkeepers and teachers, they were not considered scholars.

So the order of things was different in the overseas Chinese settlements. There, traders and shopkeepers were the top drawer, and wealth was the gauge of social worth. If you aspired to anything, you aspired to becoming a merchant. You could not aspire to high officialdom under the British since, as I have already mentioned in an earlier chapter, Chinese access to high government office was limited.

Superior social status among the Chinese was thus defined more by wealth than by scholarship or public office. As a result, for all that education was prized, money counted inordinately. Besides, the immigrant experience, as I have indicated, is all about striving and making good. And the one avenue to making good in this case was making money. Although the social pecking order has since been modified by the appearance of a professional class—of lawyers, doctors, engineers, accountants, architects, teachers and civil servants—there is a hangover of older values, and the Chinese in Malaysia are still notable more for their love of gain than for their cultivation.

Say "Chinese" to a Malay ten or twenty years ago and the image of a grasping, clannish and predatory shopkeeper, a middleman who has made himself indispensable to everyone, came immediately to mind. It is an image held of the Chinese not just in Malaysia but all over Southeast Asia. Why? After all, if you said "Chinese" to a Frenchman, say, he may think of something completely different, a poor exploited peasant, perhaps, battling against bad times in the depths of the Chinese countryside.

The reason is simple: the Malay was thinking of the immigrant in Malaysia, and the Frenchman of the native in China. Immigrant minorities typically occupy an intermediate position in the general host economy; they are typically concentrated in the small business sector. Think of the Jewish population in Europe and North America, and the Indians in East Africa (and subsequently in Britain), all "middlemen minorities," to use the sociologist's term. Retail proprietorship is a classic avenue of upward mobility for immigrants, the age-old means by which a person of humble origin may hope to become an owner, and by accumulating profits achieve a degree of personal security against the uncertainties of immigrant life.

If the *kampung* Malay came across any Chinese, that Chinese was likely to be the village shopkeeper. Chinese and Malays didn't mix save in the marketplace, and in the marketplace, the Malays often got themselves into debt as a result of the Chinese willingness to give credit. It was around the shop that Chinese-Malay relations frequently revolved, which is why, I suppose, Mahathir sees fit to comment in detail on the Chinese retail business in his book. I thought some of his observations on the commercial exploitativeness of the Chinese misdirected, however, in that the great majority of the village shopkeepers he cited as examples eked out a livelihood from their business by saving hard, living frugally, keeping costs low by working family members, keeping long hours and providing a good service (including credit) to customers. It is a life that their children consciously seek to avoid. To me the perceived unscrupulousness of the Chinese did not exist at that lowly level. These people were themselves vulnerable.

There is indeed a tight Chinese nexus between wholesalers, retailers and customers, a Chinese network which outsiders find almost impossible to penetrate. Depending on how you look at them, such elements of the nexus as dialect and regional ties and family solidarity are either barriers against outside entry or in-built Chinese strengths. Mahathir discusses them in terms of Chinese exclusivity, but it is just as valid to associate them with "middleman minorities." The over-representation of immigrants in business, for example, has been noted as far afield as the U.S., where it is indicative of neither the entrepreneurial drive of the foreign-born nor the lethargy of the indigenes.

Take immigrants from the Indian subcontinent in Britain. The British stereotype of these people is of the successful, hardworking and family-minded shopkeeper battling through hard times and surviving. As has been the case with the Chinese shopkeeper, their willingness to work long hours and their tight family networks are seen as assets. Yet there is the fact that if these immigrants work long hours for low returns, it is because they have to. If they specialise in corner shops and the rag trade, both declining businesses, it is because these were the only ones they could afford to buy into. Faced with the same limited choice, white Britons would do no differently.

To sum up, there are more dimensions to Chinese competitiveness in Malaysia than the Darwinian one (of the survival of the fittest) considered by Mahathir. Historical legacy gave them a head start, but so did migration.

CHAPTER 10

THE UGLY CHINAMAN

THROUGHOUT HISTORY, there has been a tendency for a group to regard its own way of life as the norm and to lump all the rest of mankind under some deprecatory term. The ancient Greeks called all non-Hellenic peoples "barbarians," the Hebrews labelled others as "gentiles," Muslims branded non-Muslims as "infidels," the English term foreigners (especially non-white ones) "wogs" and so on.

The Chinese are no different. That they call Europeans "foreign devils" is well known. Less widely known is their historical term for the Japanese, "dwarfs." But these are just two of the many names, generally translated as "barbarian," which they use of the non-Chinese. These names arose early in China's history, when the country was a fraction of its size today and large areas of what we know as China were inhabited by border tribes. It was to these tribes that the various names were applied.

Some of these names are still in use, though not always in the sense of "barbarian"—the word *fan*, for example, merely signifies foreign or non-Chinese origin when it appears as a prefix in the Chinese term for "tomato," *fanqie*, literally "non-indigenous eggplant." Furthermore, connotations change over time. For instance, as used today, the label "foreign devil" has little or none of the abusiveness it had when it was applied to the Westerners who arrived in China in the 19th century. When I refer to somebody as a "foreign devil," I certainly don't have any demons or evil spirits in mind. In fact, "foreign devil" can even be a term of affection.

Yet, for all that their content changes, the terms remain. To this day, a Malaysian Chinese can be heard using the word *fan* of a Malay. What does he mean, I am often led to wonder—does he really think the Malays uncultured (and he himself, by implication, civilised)? What meaning is he imparting to that word? Does he realise what he is saying? Is it just unconscious habit, or is it conscious name-calling? Is he being unthinking, or intentionally abusive?

Whatever the answers to these questions, there is no doubt that at bottom there is a persistent belief in the myth of Chinese superiority. This sense of superiority rests on the idea of a superior civilisation. It is beyond me, and the scope of this book, to describe what that civilisation consists of; suffice it to note that one of its defining elements is the early existence of a written language. We can perhaps appreciate the centrality of the written language in the Chinese scheme of things when we gaze at a work of calligraphy.

China is the ancient source of one of the world's great areas of civilisation, the area now called East Asia, which includes Japan, Korea and Vietnam. It was the ideas, beliefs and cultural achievements of China that inspired and shaped the humanities of these countries. Chinese civilisation was later threatened by the West's stronger mission to civilise, but before the 14th century, China was scientifically and technologically ahead of Europe; indeed, it was not only the richest and most powerful country in the world but, according to the Venetian visitor Marco Polo, the most civilised. He wrote of "the polish, courtesy, and respectful familiarity" which distinguished Chinese social intercourse. "Quarrels, blows, combats and bloodshed, then so frequent in Europe, were not witnessed .... Honesty was everywhere conspicuous."

If all this was the case, then why does Mahathir write in *The Malay Dilemma*—and here he is reflecting the views of large numbers of Malays—that "In [Chinese and Indian] lives, nobility which is always associated with breeding, was totally absent"? Is it because up to the time of writing he had met only ill-bred Chinese? I'd say that it was more than likely. I myself see little evidence of refinement among the Chinese in Malaysia.

Mahathir puts this down to their having come from an overpopulated country. This is clearly wrong, because if originating in an overcrowded country were the cause, then every person of Chinese descent, whether he lives in China, Hong Kong, California or New Zealand, would be ill-mannered—which is obviously not the case. What is true, though, is that while many Chinese harbour the highly refined and artistic tastes of the old scholar class, there has always been a huge gulf between the achievements of that class (which can be seen in the brilliant works of art displayed in museums and art galleries throughout the world) and the impoverished cultural life of the ordinary masses.

Furthermore, Marco Polo was describing China during one of the most glorious periods of its history. But all civilisations rise and decline, and the greatness of Chinese civilisation belongs to a long faded past. The Chinese view of the world—with themselves as central (the Middle Kingdom), and all others as peripheral—has been out of date for centuries. Today China is a Third World country trailing behind Malaysia on many measures of national well-being. Just as the Britain that created the largest empire the world has ever seen is today a second-tier European power, so the fact that China boasts the world's longest continuously recorded history now avails it little.

In Malaysia, Chinese superiority also rests on the notion that the Malays are culturally inferior, but this is an unfounded belief based on ignorance of Malay history. The ancient Kingdom of Melayu (Malay) was already in existence as early as the 5th century with records showing it as having sent tribute to China then. How long before that it was established is still unclear but it certainly preceded the Sriwijaya empire, which was centred on Palembang in Sumatra and came into prominence in the 7th century as "the Great Malay Kingdom of Sriwijaya," Sriwijaya was such a powerful empire that for 600 years, it controlled the other kingdoms of Sumatra as well as the whole of the Western Archipelago. At the height its influence extended from the waters of North Vietnam to the east and the island of Madagascar to the west.

The sultanate of Malacca, dating from 1400, was a considerable political and maritime power in Southeast Asia as well as the main diffusion centre of Islam. To picture the Malays as a contented peasantry is quite mistaken. There is insufficient awareness, writes Khoo Kay Kim, Professor of Malaysian History at the University of Malaya, that "Malay society, until at least the mid-18th century, was maritime rather than agrarian in character." It was the coming of the British traders and the opening up of Penang and Singapore as international ports which eclipsed the importance of the Malay ports. The maritime past of the Malays still lives on in the pirates-cum-traders who sail in the high seas of Southeast Asia today. These daring seafarers contradict the stereotype of the Malays as passive rural folk.

The misreading of Malay courtesy and self-effacement as Malay weakness and inferiority has earlier been mentioned. Mahathir blames the Malays themselves, their unwillingness to speak up, for the low regard in which other people held them, but Chinese insensitivity is also partly responsible for the consistent misinterpretation.

The attitude that one's own culture is special is of course not peculiarly Chinese (the Jews, for example, consider themselves a Chosen people), but the Chinese have it to a far greater degree than most people, certainly far more than the Malays. What's more, it is an attitude assumed by the least educated Chinese, those who have little knowledge of the civilisation to which they lay claim and even less access to its higher achievements.

Instead of shedding their feeling of superiority when they migrated to Malaya, the Chinese found it reinforced by the colonial order of things. In that order, they were placed above the indigenes. The social structure—with the white man at the top, the Chinese in the middle, and the Malays at the bottom—was taken for granted and considered right and proper. Not only that, but the social pecking order was taken to be a reflection of racial and cultural hierarchy. The Malay's lower social status was seen to betoken a natural inferiority. Of course, the Chinese already thought the Malays inferior, but the colonial social arrangement certainly did nothing to discourage them in this opinion.

Their attitude to the whites was more ambivalent. China had begun by expecting kowtows of all foreign emissaries. But it was forced to revise its world view by a series of humiliating defeats in the 19th century—not only at the hands of Western powers but, worse still, at those of the Japanese. There was some recognition that the West had superior methods and technology, but not necessarily superior social institutions and philosophy. There was admiration, but also contempt, and a hostility born of wounded pride.

At any rate, the immigrant Chinese found it easier to accept domination by the white man than by the Malay. It is one thing to be bossed around by a people with superior technology, quite another to be ruled by those they consider their cultural inferiors. The Chinese may accept the political supremacy of the Malay, but in their hearts they believe that theirs is the superior culture. This arrogance has resulted in some blind spots and an inability or unwillingness to give credit where due.

They consistently underestimate Malay capability, in spite of such evidence to the contrary as the increasing number of academically excellent Malay students. They are reluctant to concede that the Malay leadership has been very skilled and competent in its political, economic and social management of the country. Indeed it can be argued that since Independence Malaysia has managed better than Britain, our one-time colonial master.

Yet it is seldom to the Malays that Chinese or Indians attribute Malaysia's success. They would rather seek an explanation in the administrative foundations laid by the British or in the fact that until recently there were still a number of non-Malays among the top civil servants. Standards have been falling, they can't resist adding, just wait for the collapse! Such is their prejudice that if things went wrong, these non-Malays would say, "What can you expect, with Malays in charge?" But when things go right, it is invariably for reasons other than good Malay management.

The Chinese tendency to belittle Malay capability and achievement has manifested itself in ludicrous ways. To give just one example, when Mahathir underwent heart bypass surgery in Kuala Lumpur in 1989, it was rumoured that Lee Kuan Yew was so worried that the Malay doctors would not be up to the task that he offered to send some surgeons from Singapore to assist at the operation. The operation was successfully performed by young Malay surgeons, but rumour had it that it was in fact done by physicians flown in from the United States.

Malay success is always ascribed to the privileges and special support they get under affirmative action, but non-Malay achievement is invariably put down to innate ability and hard work. Yet it is not as though all non-Malay success is predicated on merit and application. Have the Chinese forgotten all those licences, concessions and contracts that they have won through patronage, connections and bribery? In the early stages of privatisation a Chinese group made a big killing by obtaining one of the country's most lucrative privatisation licences. The head of the group claimed that it had taken his family three generations to arrive at where they are today, whereas the Malays would get there instantly, neglecting to mention that the family business was an insignificant one until it secured a lucrative project under the NEP privatisation measures. Of the five Malaysian (four Chinese and one Indian) U.S.-dollar billionaires on *Forbes* 2002, I think most people would agree that probably not more than a couple would have done it without the benefit of a government franchise. The Chinese are quick to devalue Malay success, partly to magnify their own achievement, and partly from a reluctance to entertain the very idea of being surpassed by Malays.

They would do well to try looking at themselves through Malay eyes. Though he is probably too polite to say so, a Malay takes a low view of Ugly Chinaman qualities. These qualities include crassness, dirtiness and corruption. The popular image of the Malaysian Chinese is indeed rather coarse. As I note in the previous chapter, the more refined scholar class has never been represented in the immigrant communities, made up well into our own times of artisans and traders. Though there is now a professional and business class, its members are new-rich and it will be another generation before their manners acquire refinement and polish.

This is in some contrast to the composition of Malay society, with its kings, princes, nobles, civil servants, religious leaders and teachers, and peasants. Until recently, there were only two broad divisions in Malaysian Chinese society, merchants and those who aspired to be merchants, whereas Malay society is more rounded and more finely layered.

I can never watch the proceedings of the UMNO general assembly on television without being impressed by the splendour, oratory and wit on display. Those of the other races pale by comparison. Similarly, it is my impression that Malay interviewees on television are more articulate and coherent than the Chinese ones.

Another telling way of contrasting the two races is to juxtapose a Malay *kampung* house with a Chinese village dwelling. This says something about the personal habits, priorities, practices and, by extension, the shaping historical circumstances of the two peoples. A Malay *kampung* house is neat and picturesque, whereas a Chinese home gets to look like a disorderly workshop in no time. In the urban areas too the Malays are more house-proud than the Chinese.

Conditions inherited from centuries of overpopulation and poverty underlie some of the worst habits of the Chinese. Our tolerance for noise, untidiness and even filth must be among the highest of any people. We are noisy because living under crowded and disorderly conditions encourages noisiness. We are untidy because life is enough of a struggle as it is without having to spend time and energy on keeping up appearances. It doesn't bother us if our kitchens, say, are a mess. Is this because we are so practical-minded that we see no point in keeping a kitchen clean and tidy when it is soon going to be greasy and untidy again? As with kitchens, so with toilets. Even Singaporeans, who fancy themselves as the Swiss of Asia, have to be persuaded to flush their toilets after they have used them by the threat of a government penalty. China's lavatories are so notoriously dirty that Li Peng, the former Chinese premier, is said to have asked why a nation capable of launching satellites can't keep its toilets clean.

When I think of Chinese disorderliness, many images come to mind. One is the Malaysian Chinese cemetery, where there are no defined paths going through the tombstones and hardly any maintenance, and where the overgrowth is still cleared by burning. The other is the smelly and clotted drainage system in many Chinese neighbourhoods, including some areas in Penang, supposedly the showcase of old Chinese wealth. A third image is of Chinese weddings, where the guests are apt to be improperly attired, unpunctual and inattentive to the speeches or ceremonies, posing such a contrast to the uniformly well-dressed attendees and their punctilious observance of ritual at a Malay wedding. Another aspect of the Chinese behaviour which I find embarrassing as a Chinese is the way many jump queue and pile their plate with food and even take away food at "open house" functions hosted by government leaders and at company annual general meetings.

Men unmodified by the conditions of particular environments do not exist. The conditions under which they have lived historically have been such as to persuade the Chinese that you can't trust anyone. It is to this distrust that I attribute an important difference between the Chinese and the Japanese. The Japanese are proof that there is strength in unity. The Chinese, by contrast, are ill-disposed to cooperation; instead of working with one another, they shun working together.

The Chinese distrust of the law has also been remarked by many. Nor is theirs only distrust, but also disrespect. How can you have any respect for the law, they probably reason, when its enforcers are corrupt? Perhaps their historical experience of nepotism and official corruption is too deep for them to put much store by public probity. "After three years in a position of authority," goes an old Chinese saying, "even an upright official is enriched."

No man is beyond price, is how they look at the world. When they are faced with an obstacle in their business dealings, the first solution to pop into their heads is to grease the palm of someone. Baksheesh may be a natural part of commerce, but does it have to raise as few moral doubts as it does among the Chinese?

Of course it would be absurd to suggest that the Chinese have a monopoly on corruption in Malaysia, or that corruption is a peculiarly Chinese characteristic. Hands up anybody who can think of a scandal-free government. "Cronies," "money politics," "Commission of Inquiry"—these terms remind us that crime and bribery in high places know no cultural boundaries. What I am trying to get at is an attitude, a mindset which takes corruption for granted. And my point is that the Chinese are more given to that attitude than many other peoples.

Wherever there are overseas Chinese communities, there is organised crime—gambling, kidnapping, drugs, prostitution and protection rackets. Secret societies and criminal syndicates like the Triads are part of the very fabric of immigrant Chinese society. In Hong Kong, for example, Triad tentacles have penetrated to the topmost circles of "legitimate" business. And the entertainment industry there would be unrecognisable if you removed the Triad element from it. The Chinese habitually prey on their own kind, and when it comes to settling scores or exacting revenge they have no qualms whatsoever about taking the law into their own hands. That said, it must nonetheless be conceded that as a group they are extremely governable. They don't make much trouble but like to keep the peace.

In private, many Chinese will not think my criticisms too harsh. But their public reaction would be another matter. When Bo Yang, a dissident and renowned writer in Taiwan, wrote some essays (collected under the title, *The Ugly Chinaman*) describing certain flaws of Chinese character, he found himself roundly condemned by many of his countrymen. And what had he said? Merely that the Chinese are noisy, rude, uncivil, unruly and prone to corruption—all aspects of Chinese behaviour one encounters every other day. I didn't think when I read the book that he had said anything to get worked up about. So why the fuss? Why are Bo Yang's critics so prickly?

It is because he has touched a core of unease in the Chinese, an unease born of the contradiction between historical belief and reality—the belief in Chinese superiority on the one hand, and the reality of European challenge to that superiority on the other. These critics would not have been so defensive if they had been surer of Chinese superiority.

That sense of superiority was shattered, or at least greatly undermined, by the experience of humiliation, defeat, impoverishment and national decline. Once the world's most advanced nation, the Chinese suddenly found themselves one of the world's most backward. And they have never quite transcended the shock of this discovery. So theirs is the defensiveness of a people whose anciently inherited feelings of superiority are constantly undercut by more recently acquired feelings of inferiority.

Much cultural baggage, then, stands in the way of a change of Malaysian Chinese attitudes to Malays. That there is clearly an attitude of mind and heart that needs correcting is true of not only the Chinese but also the Indians. On the whole life has been good to them in Malaysia, but the non-Malays have trouble acknowledging that. I sometimes wonder how they would have fared in Hong Kong, Taiwan, China or India. Would they be any better off? If it is only the Malays who are holding them back, then they should be able to flourish where there are no Malays to stand in their way. Yet Malaysian Chinese migrants to Australia, Britain and North America don't strike me as having done all that well for themselves.

You still hear some Chinese and Indians say how good things were back in the old colonial days. How fair the British were when it came to the treatment of the different races. Yet the British were the ones who had the best and the biggest part of the pie. The Chinese and Indians had to make do with what was left after the British had helped themselves. As for the Malays, they were left with the tiniest portion of all. If this was fair, then heaven help us! Do they not feel any irony, these Chinese and Indians who have supplanted the British in terms of their share of the pie, when they speak of British fairness and Malay unfairness? Are they wilfully blind, or is it that their prejudice has clouded their view?

It astonishes me to remember how we cheered when white American cowboys killed and slaughtered Red Indians on movie screens. What could we have been thinking of? That it was right and proper for whites to triumph? What made us identify with the whites rather than with their victims? What made us think they were the good guys, the Indians the bad? The white colonisation of the Americas and Australasia entailed the massacre, enslavement and cultural genocide of many indigenous peoples. And still it is the whites we cheer. It is the whites we'd rather be ruled by. So distorted are our perceptions. So thoroughly are we brainwashed. So much, indeed, has white Hollywood got to us.

CHAPTER 11

MINORITY EXPERIENCES COMPARED

MY ATTENTION was recently drawn to a study entitled *Minorities at Risk: A Global View of Ethnopolitical Conflicts*, published by the United States Institute of Peace in 1993. This is a survey, said to be unprecedented, of more than two hundred politically active communal groups across the world and an examination of their disadvantages and grievances. Among other things, it ranks the degree of economic discrimination suffered by a minority on a four-point scale, with a score of 1 denoting low severity of discrimination, and a score of 4 denoting high severity.

It interested me to find the Chinese in Malaysia given a score of 4 and the Malays in Singapore a score of 2. The legend for 4 reads, "Public policies (formal exclusion or recurring repression or both) substantially restrict the group's economic opportunities in contrast with other groups," whereas 2 indicates that there is "No social practice of deliberate exclusion. No formal exclusion from economic opportunities," but also "no public policies aimed at improving the group's material well-being." In point of the severity of economic discrimination, the Chinese in Malaysia rank with the black Africans of South Africa.

How downright misleading, I thought, and how frequently the world misjudges Malaysia. We Chinese in Malaysia are said to suffer twice as much economic discrimination as do the Malays in Singapore, and yet I am far from alone in thinking that I'd rather be a Chinese in Malaysia than a Malay in Singapore. What yardstick did that survey use? How about using this yardstick: the fact that Malays are over-visible in low-paid jobs in Singapore, such as that of cleaner, driver and guard, and their conspicuous underrepresentation in the professional and business ranks? What then does that tell us about the structure of opportunity in Singapore?

If their economic opportunities had been so severely restricted by the prevailing public policies, would the Chinese poor in Malaysia have seen their numbers reduced to a fourth of what they were at the start of those policies? That reduction, the reader may remember from an earlier chapter, was achieved in the years between 1973 and 1987, when these policies were in full swing.

Some Chinese would no doubt say that the reduction was achieved in spite of, and not because of, these policies. Or that were it not for these policies, the reduction would have been even larger. Among the non-Malays, there is always the feeling that they could do better. But do better where? I am always tempted to retort. As a group, where else but in Malaysia could they have done as well?

Yet the survey by the Institute of Peace is by no means alone in seeing the Chinese as greatly disadvantaged victims. Indeed the Malaysian government is periodically accused of being racist towards its minorities. By what criterion is Malaysia judged racist? Clearly not by the fact that police brutality of the kind suffered by blacks in the U.S. is unknown to Malaysian Chinese. It is judged solely by the fact of its positive discrimination policies and not by what I think are more appropriate yardsticks, such the material betterment of all its communal groups and its record of racial accommodation.

For it is no mean feat to hold such a country together. The inflammable elements are many. The very mix of races, their numbers and their disparities make for volatility. The potential for conflict is there, and yet the country has enjoyed peace and stability for more than a quarter of a century. The high degree of racial tolerance it has displayed probably makes it unique. For in no continent in the world is communal conflict absent. The former Yugoslavia is just the most terrible of dozens of societies devastated by ethnic violence. Set against a global background, in a comparative perspective, Malaysia appears positively to radiate harmony. In fact, contrary to conventional opinion, I would say that in terms of race relations Malaysia is a success story.

To those Chinese and Indians who grumble about their lot as minorities, my advice is, "Look at other multiracial societies." Let us take a case that bears a close resemblance to that of the Chinese in Malaysia. Let us look at East Africa, where Indians have played a rôle analogous to that of the Malaysian Chinese, namely the role of a "middleman minority."

Just like the Chinese in Southeast Asia, the Indians in Kenya, Uganda and Tanzania look back to a history of coastal trading that predated the arrival of the colonial Europeans. Just like the Chinese in Southeast Asia, they came as traders and only very few stayed on as settlers. And just as has happened in Southeast Asia, all this changed when a labour market was created by European colonisation and development. Specifically, the building of the Mombassa to Uganda Railway by the British at the turn of the century caused 32,000 indentured Indian labourers to be brought over from Gujarat and the Punjab. When their contracts expired, many of these Indian labourers decided to stay on and set up businesses. With British encouragement, their numbers were added to by fresh migration from India after World War II.

Just like the Chinese in Southeast Asia, they prospered as shopkeepers, merchants and craftsmen. Certain sectors of the economy, such as wholesale, retail, import and services, came to be dominated by them. All this is quite typical of middlemen minorities. If the Indians interacted with the indigenous Africans, it was at the shopkeeper-customer level, or else it was as master and servant. They kept very much to themselves, looking down on the Africans, whom they considered culturally inferior and lazy.

They were bystanders rather than active participants in the black nationalist movements that helped win East Africa self-government. When Independence came—and here the Indian response diverges from that of the Chinese in Malaya—many of them sat on the fence and hesitated to take out local citizenship. The Chinese, on the other hand, had been very keen to acquire Malaysian nationality, so much so that they were willing to pay a price for it, that price being their agreement to the special Malay privileges written into the Constitution of the newly independent state.

But many of the Indians in East Africa were less than wholehearted in their support of the newly independent governments, fearing policies such as nationalisation and Africanisation. Yet to the newly independent black Africans, the social and economic structure left over from the colonial period—with the Europeans at the top, the Indians in the middle, and the indigenes right at the bottom—was altogether unacceptable. And they were encouraged in their perception of Indians as wealthy unscrupulous exploiters when the latter demurred at adopting local nationality, no doubt because they were uncertain about how they would fare under African rule and would rather wait and see. To the African, this careful weighing of pros and cons smacked of the very quality for which he disliked the Indian—that wish to have the best of all worlds and the obligations of none.

There are echoes of the Malay dilemma in the African dilemma. Kenyan Africans, for instance, saw their country as "the appendage of the European and Asian dominated economy." The government pledged to correct the imbalance, "so that explosive trends in race relations can be nipped in the bud by creating a more equitable society." Otherwise, it was noted in Tanganyika (now Tanzania), it would be like "sitting on dynamite." What was necessary was the creation of a class of African businessmen who could compete with the other races. This entailed large shifts of income and assets from non-Africans to Africans.

All this must sound very familiar to Malaysians. What is not so familiar is what happened to the Indians. For a time in the 1970s, the future of Indians in Africa, particularly those who had not opted for naturalisation, looked bleak indeed. Thousands in Kenya saw their shops confiscated. Large numbers left the country for good, returning to India or Pakistan, or turning to a third country, chiefly Britain, whose passports they held. In Tanzania, as part of the nationalisation of business, the Indians had their stake in the economy drastically cut back. Worst of all, they were forced to abandon their businesses in Uganda and, as is well known from the headlines of the time (1972), were thrown out of the country by Idi Amin with little more than the shirts on their backs. Uganda's economy collapsed, one reason African attitudes to Asians have since softened.

Perhaps an even closer analogy is Fiji, where the Indian immigrant population has stood to the indigenous Fijian islanders rather as Chinese have stood to Malays in Malaysia. Fiji began to excite the interest of European traders as a source of sandalwood and beche-de-mer (the sea slugs much prized in China). Then it was successively developed as a cotton, copra and sugar economy, this last by mainly Australian capital. It was colonised by Britain in 1874, and it was a British colonial governor who, drawing upon his experience in Trinidad and Mauritius, began the mass importation of Indian indentured labour, giving to Fiji the racial complexion familiar to us in Malaysia.

The numbers of Indians brought in were large, and by the end of World War I they formed no less than 30 per cent of the population. When their indenture contracts expired many of these Indian labourers set up small businesses, chiefly in the wholesale and retail sectors and in public transportation. Thus they were well on their way towards becoming a "middleman minority." By the end of World War II, the Indian population had exceeded that of the Fijian.

As had happened in Malaya, concern was expressed about immigrants overwhelming and swamping indigenes. The British recognised the need—familiar phrase!—"to safeguard the interests of the natives." The matter was debated in the Legislative Council, where those who championed the

Fijian cause played on the theme of predatory Indians keeping Fijians down while those who defended the Indians described them as frugal, industrious people whose efforts generated the wealth that gave to Fijians the chance for material advancement and security.

As Fiji moved towards Independence in the 1960s, many Fijians gave voice to their frustrations and anti-Indian feelings. The dominant theme was the economic disadvantage of the Fijians. But the transition to self-government was smooth, predicated as it was on a multiracial sharing of power by the major races. In 1966 a political organisation embracing the idea of multiracialism was launched. This was the Alliance Party, which won state power when Fiji gained Independence from Britain in 1970 and held it until the dramatic turning point in the country's fortunes in 1987.

From the outset the Fijian-dominated Alliance Party pledged to draw the predominantly rural Fijians into business and develop an indigenous capitalist class. The means to this end consisted of various preferential policies in education, employment, commerce and finance. For a variety of reasons these policies failed in their aims and the sense of Fijian disadvantage—and, by implication, of Indian economic dominance—deepened. In fact, the vast majority of the Indian population was poor and working class. Nonetheless, "Indian success/Fijian failure" was how the picture appeared to most indigenes. Although it was not Indian but Western capital which wielded the greater power in Fiji, Fijians were anti-Indian rather than anti-European.

Fijian grievance found a channel in the Taukei Movement (Taukei refers to the indigenous Fijians and the movement takes its name from the phrase *Taukei ni qele*, Fijian for "*Bumiputera*"). The movement had "Fijian paramountcy" for a slogan. In hindsight we can see that trouble was bound to come, but at the time what happened next took the world by surprise. What happened next was a military coup that overthrew the democratically elected government on May 14, 1987. Its professed aim was the removal of "the Indian threat."

Basic human rights were violated, Indians were terrorised, the economy was disastrously shaken, and political chaos descended on a country hitherto looked upon as a model of stable and democratic government.

A scenario from which, thankfully, we have been spared in Malaysia. Could it have happened here? Why not? Many of the ingredients are the same. Yet our story has turned out differently—it has turned out far more happily, thanks in no small part to the speedy narrowing of the economic cleavage between the races. As I said, in point of race relations Malaysia is a success story, and it is high time it were recognised as such.

You would come to the same conclusion if, instead of comparing them to migrant Indians, you compared Malaysian Chinese to other Southeast Asian Chinese. Take Indonesia, for instance. There the Chinese lost the battle to preserve their own cultural distinctiveness, were made to give up their Chinese names and their desire for Chinese-language education. And as the hardships that came in the wake of the Asian financial crisis in 1997 sparked off rioting in Jakarta and other Indonesian cities, the Chinese were among the first to be scapegoated and victimised, their homes, shops and businesses looted and torched, their women raped. Take also Thailand, long regarded by all as a shining example of tolerance towards its Chinese minority. It is the one place in Southeast Asia, everyone says, where the Chinese are not discriminated against. Everyone describes it as a model of racial harmony. Everyone applauds the Thais for their successful assimilation of the Chinese into Thai society. The Chinese, everyone says, gladly think themselves Thai.

And why do they think themselves Thai? There are several reasons but one of them is that they speak Thai as their first language. And why do they speak Thai as their first language? Because Chinese schools, seen to be hotbeds of Chinese nationalism, were closed down by the Thai authorities in the 1940s and the Chinese language was all but suppressed. The British in Malaya never went as far as that (their response to local nationalism was the opening of more English-language schools), and neither does the Malaysian government.

Now it has been argued that if the Malaysian government tolerates Chinese attempts to preserve their culture, it is because the Chinese minority there is uniquely large and any government would think twice about antagonising so sizeable a constituency. In other words, a government can have its way with a small minority but not with a large one.

There is some validity to this argument, and it is certainly true that the sheer weight of numbers puts the Malaysian Chinese community in a class of its own. But isn't it also the case that the larger the size of the minority, the greater the likelihood of anxiety and antagonism on the part of the majority? You don't feel threatened by—and therefore you don't retaliate against—an insignificant alien presence. It is when that alien presence increases beyond a certain magnitude that anti-foreign sentiments are called forth. Viewed in that light, the Malays appear unusually tolerant. There is strength and political leverage in numbers, but there is also vulnerability. Given Chinese numbers, it is a wonder that policies towards them are not more restrictive.

What happened in Fiji in May 1987 may remind some of the May 1969 riots in Malaysia. About 190 people died in the Malaysian conflict, but the clash did not escalate, nor has it been repeated. Indeed, on a world scale, and in a comparative perspective that includes such civil warfare as that between Croats and Serbs, or between Armenians and Azerbaijanis, or between the Sri Lankan government and Tamil rebels, what happened here appears as only a minor case of communal turbulence.

Malaysia appears as a success story even when compared to the advanced Western democracies. Before you dismiss this as a preposterous assertion, let me ask how you would describe a country where immigrants frequently suffer arson attacks on their homes, some of them resulting in fatalities? Would you not say that that was not a very tolerant country? And wouldn't you say that it was a less tolerant country than one where such attacks never occur?

Well, Britain is a country where such attacks (chiefly against immigrants from the Indian subcontinent) are persistent and where racially motivated assaults according to one recent report number more than 30,000 a year, whereas racial harassment of this kind is entirely unknown in Malaysia. Yet it is Britain, not Malaysia, which enjoys a high world reputation for tolerance. If this says anything about the way the world looks at race relations, it is that there is something the matter with it.

True, minorities in advanced democracies enjoy the same civil and political rights and benefit from the same educational, social and political opportunities as the majorities, whereas such is not the case in Malaysia. But does this necessarily mean that Malaysia is a more racist country? Imagine what would happen if gangs of Malay youths engaged in "Chink bashing" the way white youths in Britain engage in "Paki bashing." I know what would happen. The Western world would be outraged, the spectre of race turbulence would be raised in its newspapers, and doubts would be cast on Malaysia's stability. Yet "Paki bashing" in Britain goes more or less unnoticed. Am I not right to wonder if something is amiss?

Which minority is more "at risk"? Who is more "under threat"? The Chinese in Malaysia, or the Pakistanis in Britain? To me the answer is obvious. I know that many readers will reject the parallel, but it is when we allow cases which are normally kept separate to play against each other that we are made aware of the need to question the "system of ideas" by which the West describes the rest of mankind, and which we, consciously or, more often, unconsciously, adopt as our own. For there is no question that the West is the more powerful shaper of opinion, indeed of the very concepts with which we arrive at an opinion, anywhere.

When Americans and Australians, two of the most vocal on the world stage, pronounce on the racism of others, they are not necessarily being hypocritical; they may well believe in all sincerity that there is only one kind of racism—"theirs." They take that as given. Indeed they take many things as given which we are only beginning to question. By about World War I, something like 85 per cent of the earth was held by Europe as colonies, dependencies, protectorates, dominions and commonwealths. Is it any wonder that Europeans were the ones who set the rules for all other peoples?

Take terra nullius, the concept underlying the international law which allowed Europeans to take possession of the lands they "discovered." That laws says that the consent of the indigenous inhabitants was not necessary if the lands were not used, tilled, built upon or governed by a recognisable system. Based on that law, Australia was terra nullius, free for the Europeans to take without asking the Aborigines, who, as a hunting and nomadic people, were deemed by law to have neither sovereignty nor tenure over the land.

Overturning that rule in 1992 involved a tortuous wrangle through the courts. Many a legal nicety had to be examined and argued. Yet a black or brown observer whose mind has not been moulded by the European way of thinking may well wonder, utterly bemused, what all that weighing of evidence was about, since it is patently clear to him that he can't be expected to abide by a rule made by white men for other white men; that an international rule is not an international rule when it is made unilaterally.

To declare that Australia was terra nullius, a land belonging to no one because neither ownership nor political organisation in the European sense existed, allowed the British not only to annex it but to do so with right on their side, with what they considered perfect legitimacy. The "consent of the natives," embodied in the kind of treaties made with the sultans of Malaya, for example, was not needed. So far as the British were concerned, theirs was an unassailable legal position recognised by other members of "the family of nations." The trouble is, that family of nations did not include any group in the non-European world, not even, say, China (whose highly sophisticated political organisation long antedated that of any European country), let alone the Aboriginals.

The characteristically Western concern for legitimacy, for the rule of law, is all to the good, because we need to play by the rules if we are to co-exist agreeably. But still it has to be borne in mind that when a Western nation cries foul at a non-Western country, we mustn't automatically assume that it has the moral high ground or that the other party is in the wrong. There is nothing all that unassailable about many a legal position adopted.

Let me illustrate this with the case of Hong Kong. Shortly after China demanded the return of Hong Kong (ceded to Britain in the 19th century at gunpoint, under what are called "unequal treaties"), the then prime minister Margaret Thatcher made her celebrated remark that "unequal treaties" were valid in international law, and added aggressively, by way of crying foul, "If a country will not stand by one treaty, it will not stand by another."

How was the Chinese government supposed to take that remark—that if the "unequal treaties" were not respected by China, then Britain would not enter into any agreements with it? That, unlike Britain, China was not a respecter of the law? Similarly, if an Aborigine were to reject terra nullius, is that to be taken as signifying a lack of respect for international law?

I think it telling that only as recently as 1967 were Australian Aborigines granted full citizenship and counted in the national census, following a referendum. Before that date they were subject to the special laws made by the individual state governments and left out of the population statistics. What is so extraordinary is that enough white people were dubious about the change for the vote to have been less than unanimous.

To campaign for a "Yes" vote, said an Aboriginal activist, Maude Tongerie, "We had a body of Aboriginal people going out and speaking to the community and pleading to the public. We said, 'We are here, we have been here for a long time and for God's sake, somebody look at us, accept that our colour is different. We are human beings and we want self-management'." I think if I were Australian I'd think twice about accusing others of racism, lest I invite the retort that it's a case of the pot calling the kettle black. There has been no Malay equivalent, after all, to the politician Pauline Hanson, who is by no means the only Australian to oppose Asian immigration and Aboriginal rights; her racist views struck enough of a chord among her white supporters to disconcert the mainstream parties in 1998.

I have raised all these examples, from East Africa to Australia, to illustrate my point that Malaysia has acquitted itself more than creditably in its handling of race relations. The Western examples, namely Britain and Australia, should bring home to us that things are not always what they seem. That they seem that way to us is because that is how they have been represented (without necessarily any intention to falsify, it must be admitted) in the discourse of Western commentators, and because we are, to a degree we are not fully conscious of, subject to the "system of ideas" evolved by these people.

Opposition politicians, dissidents and intellectuals in Third World countries often seek validation and support for their views and struggle in the opinions of Western intellectuals. There is nothing wrong with that, but let us also maintain a critical and questioning attitude; and let us, while admiring the ideals which the West genuinely strives for—justice and honour and fair play and all the rest of it—also recognise that those who profess them do not always live up to them. Remember the contradiction between the American Creed and the reality of black exclusion pointed out by Myrdal?

The ideals themselves—of the essential dignity and equality of all human beings, of inalienable rights to freedom and justice—are admirable, and the world is a better place for them. We in Asia have much to thank the West for, but when it starts tut-tutting about our racism or human rights violations, we would be far more contrite were that disapprobation accompanied by due acknowledgement that we could tut-tut about its lapses in these matters too.

When we keep an open and sceptical mind, we may see that the non-Malays have not had a bad deal in Malaysia. To those who disagree with me, my rejoinder is, just look around the world. The lesson is clear—peace and national cohesion is better than war and disintegration. I am not saying that the non-Malays have no grounds for complaint—they have, as earlier chapters have made clear. But in grievance as in all things, it is best to have a sense of proportion.

CHAPTER 12

CULTURAL CROSSING

I ONCE asked a friend, another second-generation Chinese in Malaysia, if he thought there was a Chinese dilemma. Yes, he said, there is; the Chinese dilemma is that when we are abroad, we are Malaysians first and Chinese second, but at home, we are Chinese first and Malaysians second.

Is this the same as saying that a Chinese from China presents himself as Chinese to a Westerner, but is a Cantonese or Hokkien, as the case may be, in front of other Chinese? In other words, is it the same as saying that there are levels of identity? Not quite. "Cantonese" or "Hokkien" are important categories psychologically, but they are not significant politically, whereas "Chinese" in Malaysia counts both psychologically and politically. This comes of the communal organisation of Malaysian politics, and the fact that policies differ depending on whether you are classed as "*Bumiputera*" or "non-*Bumiputera*" (the Chinese being the biggest group in the latter category).

A Malaysian Chinese is Chinese first and Malaysian second because being differentiated from *Bumiputeras* heightens his sense of communal identity. It makes him feel that even if he wanted to, he can't not be Chinese, any more than he can choose to be Malay. You might say that in a way he is Chinese whether he likes it or not, or that he is Chinese in spite of himself: communal politics has seen to that.

But suppose he were to request admission to the Malay category? What would qualify him for membership? Obviously he would need to be converted to Islam, he would have to speak Malay as his first language, he would live like a Malay, give up his Chinese identity, intermarry, and become for all practical purposes indistinguishable from the Malays.

This may sound highly improbable to most Malaysians—how can a Chinese cease to be Chinese?—yet it has been done. The example of Sino-Thais springs immediately to mind; in Bangkok, many of those who call themselves Thais are at least partially Chinese by descent. The reverse, however, is much less likely to happen; that is, you would not find a Malay seeking absorption by the Chinese, because why would a member of the dominant group want to belong to a less dominant group?

Two conceptions underlie all majority-minority relations: the notion of the melting pot (or assimilation), and that of the salad bowl (or multiculturalism). In the one, you cast off your ethnic skin and melt into the host culture. In the other, you co-exist but stay distinct, just as tomatoes and lettuce mix in a salad bowl but remain tomatoes and lettuce. If a majority wants to see, to use George Washington's phrase, "one people" emerge from its mix of races, then it would incline towards the melting pot idea. It would demand conformity of the minorities. They would be expected to adjust, to use Mahathir's phrase in *The Malay Dilemma*, to the "definitive people." Little adjustment would be required of the definitive people themselves, except to permit the non-definitive groups to merge with them.

The melting pot idea was favoured by most Western countries—including the United States and Australia, but not Canada—until the 1960s, but then it became much less popular. Instead, there was an upsurge of interest in "roots." In any event, while assimilation has worked well enough for whites—for Irish, German or other European immigrants in America, for instance—it has been noticeably less successful in the case of more distinctly dissimilar groups, such as blacks and Asians.

The trouble with assimilation is that it has sometimes to be forced upon a minority, as has happened, for example, with the Chinese in Indonesia. The other problem is that belonging is a two-way process—you can't belong to a group that doesn't want you—and not all majorities are willing to accept minorities, particularly those it does not like, into the same melting pot.

The salad bowl idea, on the other hand, implies that groups co-exist but maintain their separate identities. In a country which professes multiculturalism, diversity in language, religion and custom is tolerated and even promoted. For instance, the right of a minority to education in its own language may receive official support or funding. Because multiculturalism means not trampling on other people's culture and suppressing their languages, it has found favour in most Western democracies. But the implications of multiculturalism are less to these countries' taste.

Multiculturalism implies the emergence of minority assertiveness. Sooner or later, this leads to the parcelling out of jobs and other desirable things on the basis of racial quotas. As I have mentioned in an earlier chapter, quotas are now under attack in the West, where backlash politics is increasingly rearing its head.

Another consequence of multiculturalism is the "cultural sensitivity" movement (another name for which is "political correctness," or PC). This embraces race, gender, homosexuality and other issues. Because of cultural sensitivity, the gender-specific word "chairman," for example, is out, to be replaced by "chairperson." Phrases like "a nip in the air" or "a chink in one's armour" are deemed racist. American Indians are Native Americans, Orientals are Asian Americans, and cripples "physically challenged." To make fun of all this, some have come up with jokes about the "aesthetically challenged" (in other words, ugly) and the "follically challenged" (bald).

One joke I've heard has the plumbing profession in England banning the word "stopcock" on the grounds that it is gender-specific and therefore sexist. The PC word is supposed to be "stop-plug." Some plumbers, goes the joke, retaliated by saying customers would be charged £18 if they wanted a new stop-plug installed but whoever wanted a stopcock could have it at the old rate of £5.

Cultural sensitivity started out as a fashion on American campuses, but it has become a matter of wider public debate, with some of its opponents attacking it as a form of censorship and even of neo-fascism. Along with the backlash against affirmative action, the attack on PC implies calling into question the very desirability of multiculturalism. A number of figures, notably the Pulitzer Prize-winning historian Arthur Schlesinger, Jr., have come out to call for a return, in effect, to the hitherto discredited idea of the melting pot or, in other words, of assimilation.

So how we think about race is as much subject to fashion as anything else. If the pendulum does swing, and America re-embraces assimilation, then it is not at all unlikely that the rest of the Western world will follow.

Though he does not call it that, Mahathir deals with assimilation in *The Malay Dilemma*. He puts it this way: to belong to Malaysia, he says, "entails identification with the definitive people," namely the Malays. Moreover, "this identification is all-pervading and leaves no room for identification with other countries and cultures. To be identified with the definitive people is to accept their history, their geography, their literature, their language and their culture, and to reject anything else." He adds that "the culture of the definitive race is perpetuated through control of language, immigration, citizenship and education."

If the Malays had been able to exercise such control from the very beginning, Mahathir writes, then a homogeneous society stamped with Malay features would have evolved. But since this did not happen, Malaysia is now more or less stuck with communalism. To put it in another way, Malaysia can't be anything other than a salad bowl. Besides, it can't not be communal when it makes a separation between *Bumiputera* and non-*Bumiputera* and practises affirmative action. Affirmative action is part of the logic of multiculturalism. Affirmative action and assimilation are mutually exclusive.

This is what the Malay journalist Rehman Rashid implies when, looking back on the NEP on its 30th anniversary, he writes in the *Far Eastern Economic Review*: "Insofar as it has succeeded, however, it has done so by entrenching a level of political separation that has made virtually two worlds of this one nation .... Malaysians today can only look at each other across a 30-year gulf of unshared experiences, uncommon ground and divergent memories: siblings separated at birth."

What does this mean for Malay-Chinese relations? Does it mean that there will be little crossing of the divide between *Bumiputera* and non-*Bumiputera*? Not necessarily. Intermarriage between Chinese and Malays not only occurs but is becoming more common. I would expect the trend to continue at a faster rate as cross-racial mingling between social and intellectual equals increases—at school, at university, at work and socially. Of course, racial consciousness can no more go away than social grouping can. The O.J. Simpson case in America showed that even when the issue is not one of race—it was murder, in this particular instance—large sections of the public responded to its outcome along racial lines. But this is not to say that we can't try to narrow the groupings' distinctiveness and aim for some overall harmony.

Does Malaysia's salad bowl politics mean that the Chinese will remain assertively Chinese forever? Not necessarily. Communal identities change with time as relationships within and between groups alter. The stronger the outside pressures on a minority and the greater its sense of disadvantage, the more intense will be its sense of separateness. Conversely, not feeling themselves "under threat" will weaken the Chinese's communal identity. Much depends, as I said, on relationships within and between the groups.

To take relationships between the groups first, Chinese grievances of the kind described in an earlier chapter have soured race relations. Recent years may have seen a decline in such cases, but a sense of injury lingers, often outlasting its cause by a long period. It takes a very philosophically minded person to shrug off discrimination. Understandably, most people simply end up antagonised against those they think have hurt their interests. All this intensifies the sense of "us" and "them."

Turning to relationships within groups, I would suppose that Chinese identity would weaken if, say, the hard core of the community were to give ground to the silent majority, and if Malay liberals were to prevail over Malay conservatives. All these shifts within groups can affect relations between groups.

Another condition contributing to the strength of Chinese identity is the extent of their cultural differences from the Malays. Of these differences, the most significant is thought to be religion. It is because Malays are Muslims and Chinese are not, most people say, that never the twain shall meet. "How can you expect the Chinese to give up eating pork?" they say. A comparison is often drawn with Thailand, where Buddhism eases rather than hinders the assimilation of the Chinese.

However, conventional wisdom does not always, or even often, equal truth. People assume the religious barrier to be a given in Malaysia, but you have only to look at China to see that being Chinese needn't be incompatible with being Muslim. Far from it. Islam has huge numbers of adherents in China, and when I say adherents, I don't just mean non-Han Chinese minorities like Tartars and Uighurs either. I mean people who speak Chinese and who are physically indistinguishable from other Han Chinese.

Admiral Cheng Ho, whose voyages are known to most Chinese in Southeast Asia, and who is even worshipped as a deity in some migrant Chinese communities, was a Muslim. Introduced by Arab and Persian traders, Islam made enormous headway in the 13th century and continues to be a vibrant faith in China today. The country boasts tens of thousands of mosques, and many towns in the northwest have an Islamic feel to them. There is a Muslim group, called Hui, who have their own autonomous province in China, but Muslims are scattered all over China, and there is scarcely a Chinese town or city that does not boast at least one pork-free *halal* restaurant. What is more, such restaurants are not seen as anything strange or exotic but are patronised by large numbers of Chinese, whether Muslim or not. And in offices, schools, factories and hospitals, Muslim Chinese staff are given an extra subsidy to meet the higher cost of eating at a Muslim restaurant if the canteens at their place of work don't offer *halal* fare.

So in itself, Islam is not unattractive to the Chinese. If it were simply a matter of religious faith, it would not be so to Malaysian Chinese either. But what complicates matters here is that Islam is part of the definition of Malay identity. Here, it is inseparable from Malayness. This renders it off-limits, in a way, a sort of closed shop, to the Chinese, because if Malayness is not something the Chinese can acquire, then neither is Islam. This view, however, is erroneous. In fact the Malays have always use the concept of "*masuk Melayu*" (become Malay) to expand Malay society regardless of ethnicity or religion. It was only in recent times and even then only in Malaysia, that Islam has become part of the requisites. Indeed, the Malaysian constitution even today does not prescribe ethnicity as part of the definition of Malay and that is how many Indians have become Malays. Therefore Chinese too can become Malays.

Another is the bad press Islam has been getting in the world at large especially after the September 11, 2002 attack on the World Trade Center. The Western prejudice against the religion probably lessens its appeal to the Chinese as well. To all too many people in the West, Islam simply means Ayatollah Ruhollah Khomeini, Osama bin Laden and Saddam Hussein. Some years ago an English author, David Mason, was paid nearly £1 million for the book and film rights to his thriller, one in which Saddam Hussein is felled by a bullet in an audacious assassination planned and carried out by British assassins. The publisher who paid the big advance was no doubt confident the book would sell because it would pander to the wish-fulfilling fantasies of the reading public, who would dearly love the Gulf War to have ended in the death of Saddam Hussein—a death brought about, what's more, by Europeans.

For so long, the West looked at the atrocities in the former Yugoslavia, the brunt of them borne by Muslims, and said that they couldn't do anything. As the war lengthened the endless list of victims and the horrors of "ethnic cleansing," the European nations shilly-shallied. Would they have acted so indecisively if the victims hadn't been Muslims?

Malaysian Chinese parents have been heard to complain that their children were required to attend classes in "moral education" where, instead of the pupils' own religion, Islamic values were propagated. But contrast this with the ready Chinese acceptance of Christian teaching and the bias against Islam becomes immediately apparent.

Underpinning those parents' complaint was a feeling that their own customs and beliefs were being eroded. That feeling was exacerbated by the increasing difficulty, as perceived by the Chinese and Indians, of obtaining land and approval for the building of places of worship other than mosques. The underlying anxiety was, "Where does this creeping Islamisation of Malaysian society leave us?"

There is no question that the older generation of Chinese are fearful of losing their Chinese identity, the markers of which in Malaysia are Chinese language and customs. They speak darkly of "cultural erosion," but while their fear is understandable enough, I wonder if they wouldn't become better reconciled to their position if I were to ask them to consider "creeping sinicisation." A question I often ask is: what would have happened if it had been the other way round and Malays were the immigrants in China, occupying a similar position to the one held by the Chinese in Malaysia? "The answer's simple," one Chinese said to me, "the Malays would have become thoroughly Chinese." In other words, they would have suffered total "cultural erosion."

Historically, the Chinese prided themselves on their ability to bring people out of barbarism to civilisation. To the Chinese it was a given that "culturally superior" people absorbed "culturally inferior" people, and that this absorption could happen even if the culturally superior ones were conquered by "barbarians." Sooner or later, the "barbarians" would become civilised (like the Chinese), and end up sinicised. Indeed there is an ancient Chinese phrase which roughly means: "Come to China and be changed for the better." It has been said half in jest that what happens when aliens settle in China is that they start making more and more exquisite porcelain.

The underlying assumption to all this is that others would find Chinese culture quite irresistible. By way of example, the Chinese often cite the Manchus who conquered China in the 17th century and founded the Qing (Ch'ing) dynasty. The Manchus were rough martial tribesmen from across China's northern frontiers. What did the founding emperor do once Manchu rule was established over China? He began the study of Confucian classics under a team of Chinese tutors and worked hard at mastering Chinese calligraphy! Though their women drew the line at footbinding, within a century the Manchus had become assimilated and had become to all intents and purposes indistinguishable from high-born Chinese.

There you are, you see, the Chinese chauvinist would say; as with the Manchus, so with the Malays: they would have become sinicised if they had settled in China. But if sinicisation is thought to be such a good thing, why is Islamisation thought to be such a bad thing? Both mean the "cultural erosion" and assimilation of the other people.

And while we are on the subject of assimilation, I should add that although it consistently occurred at the top tiers of Chinese society, the same was not necessarily true of the lower levels. There were many minorities within China's borders who resisted assimilation and remained ethnically distinct. Also, in the case of the Manchus, becoming indistinguishable from the Chinese did not stop many Chinese from seeing them still as foreign conquerors. Even after two and a half centuries of Manchu rule, those Chinese who sought to overthrow them still formulated their revolutionary goals as "avenging the national disgrace" and "restoring the Chinese."

In any event, the cultural adaptation was not one-way, and the Chinese took things from the Manchus as well. For instance, the familiar *cheongsam*, the dress with the mandarin collar and the side slits worn by Chinese women to this day, started out as a Manchu costume—in fact, the Mandarin name for it, *Qipao*, means "Manchu gown," *Qi* being another name for "Manchu." So a dress that is thought to be quintessentially Chinese is in fact foreign in origin. Another is the pigtail, worn by Chinese men until the fall of the Qing dynasty. Forced to adopt this hairstyle by the Manchus, the Chinese were faced with the stark choice between "keeping their hair and losing their heads" and "losing their hair and keeping their heads." Initially the pigtail was hated by the Chinese as a mark of national humiliation, but gradually they grew attached to it, and those who migrated abroad and could have cut it off continued to cherish it as a mark of their Chinese identity.

Cultural borrowings are inevitable when peoples live side by side. If they find the *baju kurung* attractive, Chinese girls will wear it, and they increasingly do so in Kuala Lumpur. There are Malay loan words in Chinese speech, such as *pa'nai* (*pandai*, or "clever"), and a strong Malay flavour to the Chinese food in Malaysia. We are all familiar with Chinese coffeeshops, patronised almost entirely by Chinese, with stalls selling Malay *nasi lemak* and *satay* and Indian *mee rebus*. The Chinese are not chauvinistic when it comes to good food!

The cultural diffusion is by no means one-way: for example, the Malays use the Chinese *angpow*, the New Year gift of money in a "red packet," during their own religious festivals. And they are a dab hand at making such favourite Chinese dishes as Stuffed Beancurd and Hainanese Chicken Rice.

In fact, racial loyalties are transcended in many areas of life in Malaysia. Contrary to the belief that the Chinese will only give business to other Chinese, the majority do not hesitate to seek out good Indian doctors and lawyers and, increasingly, to use Malay professional services. Today the top cardiac surgeons are Malay, and in choosing to be operated on by these men, many Chinese are putting their lives, as it were, in Malay hands. It is well known that many Malays have adopted children of other races. Lat, the Malay cartoonist, is a hero to all the races, and indeed owes much of his popularity to his lampoons against the ethnic idiosyncrasies of each group and its political personages. By mid-1999, some 60,000 Malay pupils were found to be studying in Chinese-medium schools, not necessarily because their parents wanted them to learn the Chinese language, but because they believed the teaching there to be more committed.

And surely there is no better illustration of cross-racial allegiance than the massive Chinese backing of Mahathir in the 1982 elections, the first he won as UMNO president. Abandoning the communal opposition parties, the Chinese gave their full support to Mahathir, the Mahathir of *The Malay Dilemma*! They could sense the winds of change in Mahathir's platform—a *Bersih, Cekap dan Amanah* ("clean, efficient and trustworthy [government]")—and showed that their confidence in his qualities overrode communal loyalties.

In any case, many Malays are of mixed blood. Mahathir, for example, has Indian blood, as do many other Malay leaders. His predecessor, Hussein Onn, had Turkish blood, and the Tunku, Thai. Many a Malay has quipped that, to be a successful Malay these days, you must have *darah keturunan keling* (to be of Indian descent) or *darah keturunan Arab* (to be of Arab descent) and so on. The Malays are not racial purists.

Much crossing of ethnic lines in fact goes on in Malaysian society. The cultural borders are probably particularly permeable for members of the younger generation, who are less encumbered by cultural baggage than their parents. Among these Chinese youngsters, "cultural erosion" does not elicit strong reactions.

This brings me to the subject of Chinese-language education, which will remain a thorny issue for some time to come. Here I see the increasing use of English among all the races as a solvent. The use of English by the elite of all races is a colonial legacy that has persisted in the face of the spread of Malay. Cultural identity and ancestral tongue are matters of the heart, but for most people the choice of which language to study at school comes from the head. It was a hard-headed response to the relentless pressures of economic logic that saw enrolment in English language evening classes tumble in Cantonese-speaking Hong Kong—why study the language of a power on its way out? That same logic caused the corresponding figures for Mandarin (the language of the government to which Britain handed Hong Kong over in 1997) to grow by leaps and bounds. The future of the Chinese language in Malaysia will conceivably be decided by the trade-off between the costs and benefits of maintaining it.

In summing up, I would like to argue against what is called a primordialist view of racial identity. What I am trying to say is that the markers of identity are not givens, fixed for all time. Not converting to Islam doesn't follow inexorably from Chinese identity; nor does the preference for pork. And just as Manchu accoutrements such as the *cheongsam* and the pigtail can, in the course of time, come to be seen as typically Chinese, so can Malay ones.

And vice versa.

CHAPTER 13

STRIKING A BALANCE

THE NOTION of "balance" is pleasing to almost everyone, connotating as it does a steady position and a harmony of proportion. We like our accounts to balance, we like to be of balanced mind, we like to keep our balance and not fall off, and so on. When an imbalance occurs, you would suppose that we would all want to right it.

Not so. Attempts to redress imbalances are often fraught with discord, provoking a great deal of disagreement and resistance from the side to which the balance has so far been tipped. Consider the longstanding row over Japan's huge trade surplus with the U.S. and the latter's attempts to redress the imbalance. America accuses Japan of protectionism and blocking market access to U.S. goods; the Japanese attitude, on the other hand, is basically one of, "It's your own look-out if you can't out-compete us." America's rejoinder to this is: "It's not that our merchandise is not competitive against yours; it's those structural barriers of yours against access." In other words, the Japanese are not playing fair because they are being discriminatory against U.S. goods.

This argument translates easily into the kind that has been voiced over the so-called "institutionalised" forms of discrimination. Competing for the same job, A gets it not because he is better qualified than B but because he went to Eton and Oxford and can tap into an old-boy network. The favouritism shown to Oxbridge graduates is a structural barrier or a form of "institutionalised" bias that works against B. The NEP is often condemned as a form of Malay favouritism, but isn't there a case for seeing it as making official and explicit what, in other societies, operates unofficially and covertly?

Think back to colonial times. Nowhere was it written that the plums should go to the British rather than the Chinese; and yet they did. If any Chinese objected, he would probably be given "rational" reasons like "You don't meet the necessary qualifications" or "You lack the right experience." The bias against him was not spelt out in any ground rules. With the NEP, at least you know where you are.

To go back to the question of "balance," let us consider the sizeable trade surplus that China has chalked up with the United States. For 1993, U.S. trade statistics show a figure four times that shown in the Chinese statistics. Needless to say, the difference is a source of much mistrust and finger-pointing in the two countries' trade negotiations, with the Americans accusing the Chinese of under-assessing their exports to the U.S.

You would expect a similar mistrust on the part of the Malaysian Chinese in regard to figures showing how much redressal is still needed to achieve the balance aimed for by the NEP. A couple of years before the NEP was renewed, they questioned the reliability of official estimates (The Mid-Term Review of the Fourth Malaysia Plan and the Fifth

Malaysia Plan) showing the Malay corporate share to be 18.7 in 1983 and 17.8 per cent in 1985. How can this be so, they asked, when the Fifth Plan states that "ownership by *Bumiputera* individuals grew at a fast rate of 32 per cent per annum?" It was enough to make you doubt if any of the statistics could be trusted, they said, and to encourage you in your suspicion that the Malay share had already reached the 30 per cent targeted by the NEP.

Furthermore, the Chinese claimed, the Malay share has been underestimated and the Chinese stake inflated: look at the nominee companies, they said, which mask Malay ownership; and the inclusion in the Chinese share of the amount owned by foreign citizens resident in Malaysia.

Evaluating the NEP in 1988, when it had two and a half more years to run, some members of the MCA lamented what they saw as its creation of "new imbalances." Here are the "new imbalances" they enumerated: the Malay ownership of 69 per cent of domestic banking and financial institutions; the award of 96 per cent of government scholarships for Malays to study abroad between 1980 and 1984; the allocation of only $74 million during the entire history of the New Village development under all the five Malaysia plans as against the $5 billion given in the Fourth Malaysia Plan alone for Malay-oriented land and regional development and irrigation projects; the participation of only 1.7 per cent and 2 per cent of non-*Bumiputeras* in the Felda and Felcra schemes (the government's agricultural development agencies); and the reservation of places on off-campus programmes set up with American universities for *Bumiputera* students exclusively.

As I said, "balance" is considered desirable by almost everyone, but when it comes to deciding whether something is balanced or not, disagreements often arise. A New Village Chinese may complain about the government neglect of his neighbourhood, but his perception of unfairness will not be shared by the Malay *kampung* dweller who envies that village's electricity and piped water.

There was a time when Malays emigrated out of frustration with the hassles they had in getting proper visas for their foreign spouses too. That the grouses cut across racial lines prompted Mahathir to say that the government must be doing things fairly since everyone was complaining! Even when it is just among the Malays, perfect balance is hard to achieve; why else would they say that when it comes to qualifying for Malay privileges, there are three classes of *Bumiputeras*: the *putera-puteri*, with royal blood; the UMNO-putera, with political connections; and the plain *Bumiputera*?

One can argue about fairness and unfairness till the cows come home. There is no question, though, that many Chinese feel that they have had the rougher deal. We often raise no objections to a social policy when viewed in the abstract, or on a general level. Redistributive justice? Fine, we say, laudable even. But when the policies aimed at achieving that justice hurt us on a personal or individual level, we begin to feel differently.

Many Chinese say they applaud the goals of the NEP but deplore the way it has been implemented, which they see as more biased than is necessary and also subject to abuses. Many Chinese, such as the hawker who is prevented from transferring his licence to his son, and the squatter forced off "his" land, have indeed experienced unfair dealings at the hands of some highhanded Malays. Malay resentment of the Chinese (arising, as Mahathir suggested in his book, from their dealings with Chinese shopkeepers) would seem to have been directed indiscriminately against those most easily bullied: the poor Chinese. The poor Chinese feel aggrieved by the NEP. Rightly so.

Because the Malays, through their dealings with a middleman minority, thought that the Chinese were rich, they felt resentful, forgetting the many poor Chinese who shared their plight. Their outrage was thus not balanced. This imbalance was translated into the indiscriminate highhandedness which many of us have either heard of or personally experienced. The Malay resentment of the Chinese shopkeeper was generalised to the whole Chinese community.

Mahathir noted that one reason the Malays were uncompetitive was that they knew that if they failed in the city they could always return to the *kampung* and eke out a living. But he failed to mention the obverse side of this observation: the Chinese have no Plan B to fall back on should they fail in the urban area. For them, failure would mean hardship and a hand-to-mouth existence. Their business is their only rice bowl. To threaten their food security is to give rise to their feelings of vulnerability and oppression. The Chinese may be risk-tolerant, even risk-addicted, but not with their rice bowl. To the Chinese poor, the costs of the NEP are real. And no ivory tower argument about the overall benefits will console them.

If Group X is told it should give three dollars out of its ten to Group Y because Y has nothing, it may do so willingly, but if certain members of Group Y make life difficult for some members of Group X, then all of Group X is likely to feel resentful and aggrieved. The business and professional classes in Group X may have benefited enormously from the good performance of the economy, a performance owed to sound economic management by Group Y, but when they hear of their friends or relatives being hard done by, they are not going to think well of Group Y. Any sense of gratitude they may have for the benefits they themselves have enjoyed goes out of the window.

Even without embellishing or inflating it, gossip can, merely through repetition, turn an isolated incident of unfairness into proof that the Chinese as a whole suffer Malay discrimination. Just as a single spark, Mao Zedong has famously said, can light a prairie fire, so a solitary case of unfairness can provoke a widespread sense of mistrust and grievance. The seriousness of the damage done to the goodwill among the races becomes disproportionate to that of the incident. The unfairness at the micro-level is remembered, but the fairness of the policy at the macro-level—the need to give the Malays extra help to catch up with the other races—gets lost in the general recrimination.

The rationale of the NEP was to enable the Malays to catch up, or, as Mahathir put it in his book *The Malay Dilemma*, to achieve a "levelling of the playing field." To that end, the Chinese were called to "do their bit to promote harmony." The book painted a picture of Chinese economic hegemony. By the mid-1990s, the economic scene had changed enormously. Yet, despite the high Malay representation in modern and emerging sectors such as financial services, infrastructure and communications, and the fact that Malay ownership through institutions like PNB and the various cooperatives dominated the banking, shipping, transport, telecommunications and other industries, the idea of Chinese hegemony persisted.

The Western press did not help by perpetuating myths about the overseas Chinese, the darling of Western journalists in the mid-1990s—portrayed as a transnational business empire owning colossal portions of the commercial and manufacturing assets of all the Southeast Asian countries where they are settled. A transnational empire, what's more, that will help drive China forward and shake the world. The effect of such coverage was to focus popular opinion in the various countries on the rich Chinese and deflect attention from the many more poor Chinese.

If the dominance of the Chinese in Malaysia was exaggerated, the ability of the Malays was underestimated. One has only to read *The Malay Dilemma*, especially its remarks on how the Malays might be helped to become small traders, to see by how much that ability was underestimated. Within the short span of the NEP, the Malays have risen from the *kampung* to the topmost tiers of business life. We must correct both misconceptions—about Chinese dominance and Malay laggardness—and recognise that the playing field which Mahathir thought was not level is probably now about level in many of the important sectors of the economy.

I believe the government is aware of the change. This being so, something should be initiated at the highest levels, if it has not already, to curtail those injustices which so trouble the humbler Chinese and Indians. To attain the goal of racial harmony, the government has always had to strike a delicate balance between economic restructuring (the NEP) on the one hand, and not upsetting the Chinese and Indians on the other. With the resounding success of the one, it is time to be more attentive to the other. The balance should tip towards considering Chinese grievances more.

What this means is that, since the government recognises the huge strides made by the Malays, it should scale down the NEP. Mahathir was quoted as saying in 2001 that the NEP was still necessary. But do its measures still have to be applied across the board? I think not. When there was a big gap between the Chinese and the Malay, a cold-turkey solution was necessary, but there is a much better balance today.

As a whole the Chinese have been very tolerant and done their bit to maintain good race relations. Now that the Malays are economically secure, maybe they should lift their game and set the nation's sights on not just maintaining racial tolerance but actually promoting harmony.

The Chinese are pragmatic. If you tell a Chinese that three new universities will be built to cater for Malays, he would probably just shrug. But if he satisfies the academic qualifications for admission but is displaced by a Malay through the operation of a new quota system, he is likely to feel hard done by and indignant. If you say to him, look, we have to divide the economic pie unequally to make more over to the Malays, he would probably not mind too much so long as the pie is expanding and he gets a growing slice as well.

To sum up, while the benefits of the NEP were going to the business class the price was being chiefly borne by those lower down the economic ladder. The highhandedness of petty Malay officials exacerbates the situation. Through the grapevine, individual cases of such highhandedness are foregrounded, and the larger picture lost sight of. The dramatic change in the balance of economic power should occasion a reappraisal of policy by the government with a view to toning it down. Such a move will lessen not only Chinese grievance but also the likelihood of their seeing only the racial bias and not the larger picture. A fully united and loyal nation will then not seem that far off.

CHAPTER 14

THE NEW ECONOMIC POLICY (NEP): A RECAPITULATION

BY GATHERING my thoughts under neatly labelled chapters, I may have given the impression of having tidied the complexity of my subject. I hasten to assure the reader that this is a false impression, because the subject of race relations is entangled in a confusion of dilemmas from which no single book can free it. Many abler observers than I have tackled it, but "race" is notorious for the tangles in which those attempting to discuss it are likely to enwrap themselves.

Here is Myrdal describing the literature on the problem of American blacks: "Wandering around the stacks of a good American library, one is amazed at the huge amount of printed material on the Negro problem. A really complete bibliography would run up to several hundred thousand titles. Nobody has ever mastered this material exhaustively, and probably nobody ever will. The intellectual energy spent on the Negro problem in American should, if concentrated in a single direction, have moved mountains." The mind boggles to think by how much that material has grown in the fifty-odd years since Myrdal wrote his book and by how little the problem has been ameliorated.

I must admit that when I embarked on this book, I had little inkling of the thicket of contradictory issues I was walking into. I remained convinced throughout, however, that it is possible to cut a path through this thicket.

I am relieved at least that I didn't have to walk through the library stacks described by Myrdal. In sharp contrast to the literature on black Americans, very little has been written about the race situation in Malaysia. Why is this so, apart from the smallness of our intellectual community? Some Malaysians I questioned pointed to the gagging effect of the Constitution (Amendment Act) of 1971, which prohibited public discussion of such racially sensitive issues as special Malay rights and the national language policy. This may have left the field to non-Malaysian writers, chiefly Western academics and journalists who, almost without exception, have found nothing good to say about the country's race policies. Though they try to give a semblance of impartiality, you don't even have to read between the lines to see that they are on the side of the Chinese.

Why is this the case? One reason, I think, is that they are biased towards the Chinese already. What I mean by this is that, as an object of study, the Chinese simply interest them more than other peoples. There is a large literature in European languages on the Chinese in Southeast Asia, larger probably than that on any of the other peoples in the region.

What is more, a very high proportion of this literature portrays the Chinese as a persecuted minority, making good in the face of overwhelming odds. Deep down we all have a need for heroes, and, looking around in Southeast Asia, these writers alight on the Chinese. There is also the familiar desire to champion the underdog, and again it is the immigrant Chinese who satisfy that desire. Who better to illustrate the inspirational theme of the poor immigrant lifting himself by the bootstraps and triumphing over those who would do him down? It was the Chinese of Southeast Asia (and the Jews of Europe) whom Sowell invoked to make his case against seeing failure as the result of discrimination. These are people, he says, who have prospered in the face of "centuries of injustice, punctuated by recurring outbursts of lethal mass violence."

The example of the Chinese is a very powerful weapon in the armamentarium of those who lean towards a conservative view in the longstanding debates on what society should do about poverty. The question on which the arguments mostly turn is: does the responsibility for poverty lie with society, or does it lie with the poor themselves? In other words, is there something wrong with society (injustice, an unfairness in the distribution of opportunities, etc.), or is there something wrong with the poor themselves (laziness, apathy, incompetence and so on)? The conservative inclines to the latter view, and believes that it is up to the poor to face up to the demands of society, rather than the other way round. The progressive who opposes him, on the other hand, would argue for a change in the opportunity structure in education, employment and other aspects of life.

Of course I simplify, and in reality there are many shades of grey between the positions which, by way of shorthand, I call conservative and progressive. Among us there are many, for example, who do not believe that the poor have brought poverty upon themselves but who are nonetheless bothered by the thought of people living off welfare or by the setting aside of education or employment quotas for certain sections of society. Yet, traced to its origin, this feeling of discomfort will be found to stem from the philosophy, often not admitted, that people are responsible for their own success or failure, and that society does not owe anyone a living. That Chinese success appears to be rooted in self-reliance, then, justifies the conservative in us.

Transposed to the question of race, the two positions, labelled "conservative" and "progressive" for convenience, are exemplified by Singapore and Malaysia. A comparison of the two approaches would serve to illustrate the point I am trying to make. The Malays, just short of 15 per cent of the population in 1980, are the largest minority community in Singapore. Like Malaysia, Singapore pursues multiculturalism rather than assimilation, one reason it recognises Malay as one of its official languages (the others being Chinese, Tamil and English).

But a crucial difference between the two is that, while Malaysia believes in state intervention to eliminate the identification of race with economic function (in other words, it believes in changing the opportunity structure of society), Singapore believes in the opposite route to the same objective. To eliminate race as an explanation for success or failure, Singapore believes, you have to have a strictly meritocratic system: the Malay minority is expected to make the grade "through hard work and merit." To put it in another way, Malaysia believes in changing society, while Singapore places the responsibility for change upon the individual. To paraphrase Mahathir, Singapore is saying to the Malay: "Come and get it; it's all yours if you work hard and show merit. It's up to you to face up to the demands of society. Out-compete the Chinese if you can."

If I were Malay I would reply, "How can we, the odds are stacked so high against us?" I would feel the frustration of the American exporters battling against the walls which shut them out of the Japanese market. But the issue of whether an avowedly meritocratic society is truly meritocratic is a separate issue from the one I am for the moment considering. For the moment, let us simply take meritocracy at its face value.

Singapore, in the 1980s, launched some social programmes to help its Malay minority to catch up—programmes such as the Council for the Education of Muslim Children, which provided educational aid and subsidies to reduce the dropout rate among Malay schoolchildren; and the Singapore Malay Economic Association, aimed at advancing the Malays in business and commerce. Did these projects imply a rethinking of the government's position? Not fundamentally. They were seen as self-help projects, not free lunches; while they mitigated the harshness of a meritocracy, they were not meant to compromise it. Singapore still sees itself as a meritocratic society, one whose hard edges are softened by social policies of the kind just mentioned.

Because it appears to be run on a system whose underlying philosophy is, "Let the best man win," Singapore is judged a fairer society than Malaysia by the world at large. After all, who would argue against a system which professes to reward only the deserving? Some readers may remember an American study I cited where Singapore's Malays are ranked as being a less endangered minority than the Chinese in Malaysia.

One of the ironies of Western perception is that if Singapore practised affirmative action on a larger scale, its stock will probably rise even higher. Yet Malaysia has no well-wishers for its affirmative action programmes. The paradox is, if it had done nothing for the Malays, it would probably have been censured as well. Isn't this a case of being damned if you do and damned if you don't? Of course, if a race other than the beneficiaries of the programmes held the reins of government, then I'm sure the NEP would be applauded. Were it not for the fact that they are numerically and politically superior, the Malays would be considered a deserving target for affirmative action policies.

Mahathir has said of the NEP that "No other country has tried this kind of experiment." In point of fact it is not unique—Sowell's book, for example, looks at varieties of affirmative action in India, Nigeria, Sri Lanka and the United States—but what does make it singular is its degree of success in Malaysia. Which country in the world provides better proof that poverty is not the consequence of personal or racial disabilities? I doubt if even the Malays themselves could have imagined how spectacular would be their advance under the NEP. The distribution of benefit is far from perfect, but the NEP has also made great strides in its other goal, the eradication of poverty.

In an interview in 1993, Mahathir said: "The BBC recently said we are an oppressive authoritarian country. Our people are being oppressed? Come on. We don't mind with 8 per cent growth." Whatever else you may think of the NEP, two things you can't accuse it of are depressing the economy and destabilising the country.

Things will be all right, people say, as long as the economy stays healthy, but wait till it next jumps the rails. It is true that race relations are apt to turn sour in a recession, and Chinese disaffection was perhaps at its worst during the slump of the mid- to late-1980s. Migration figures are a good indication of how people feel about a country. While Malaysian migration to Australia reached a peak in 1988-89, figures from the Australian Bureau of Immigration and Population show that the numbers dropped by more than 50 per cent between 1991 and 1992. Happy days may be here again, but what if the economy stalls as it did when Malaysia, along with other Asian countries, entered a period of sharply reduced growth and political confusion in 1998. This was the Asian financial crisis, an onslaught of shocks as the ringgit dived, the stock market tumbled, growth slowed and political fractiousness intensified. The economy had billions yanked out of it by overseas investors, and what had been termed an economic miracle came to be seen as a bubble.

There has been no shortage of explanations as to why the crisis happened and how to cure it. A widely accepted view is that international capital streamed into the Asian economies too abundantly, without due regard for the risks (the immature banking systems and securities markets), and then fled too abruptly. The over-borrowing and over-investment which resulted from the surge of capital could not go on forever. Nor could the fast growth they induced. As Paul Krugman, the celebrated American economist, has famously argued, such growth has come not from improved productivity but simply from heavy investment and increased employment.

But the deepest roots of the crisis, Western observers say, lie in crony capitalism, the "cosy" relationship between governments, banks and firms which ensures easy lending to prop up politically well-connected but wasteful and inefficient firms. In Malaysia, as in other countries these observers cite, money was allocated by the government and the banks on the basis of political connections and considerations, and so was over-invested in property and grandiose construction projects with meagre returns. An oft-cited example is Renong, a Malaysian conglomerate with interests in banking, construction, telecoms and a host of other sectors. Once the commercial arm of UMNO, the conglomerate borrowed heavily, using as collateral shares in its subsidiaries. When share prices plunged and the banks demanded more collateral, UEM, a subsidiary of Renong, bought a big stake in its own parent company. Many thought this a scandalous bailout of investors close to the government since, to make it possible, the latter had to waive stock market rules requiring a general offer to be made to all minority shareholders.

Bankrupting troubled firms—that is, not bailing them out—was one of the remedies prescribed by the IMF (together with high interest rates and government spending cuts). Failed local banks urged to bite the bullet and close down might swallow such bitter medicine with better grace if the IMF were to let multinational financial institutions face the consequences of their own miscalculated foreign currency loans to companies in the afflicted countries instead of providing these countries with emergency funds which, in effect, helped to bail out those creditors. Those international creditors got paid back, while local firms and employment suffered the savage effects—including disintegrating social order and starving people—of the IMF's policies. In this, surely, lay the real "moral hazard"? American preachiness, too, might be better received were it not seen to be hypocritical: why, if propping up failed companies is such a bad thing, was a bailout arranged to prevent the collapse of Long-Term Capital Management (LTCM), the multi-billion dollar hedge fund, whose director was a former deputy of the Reserve Board Chairman Alan Greenspan—as good an example of pure "crony capitalism" as any here. And yet to this day IMF and American officials continue to insist that afflicted countries finish their IMF medication and "crash land" while applauding Greenspan's initiatives to soft land the American economy.

If Asia is plagued by corruption, it is not as though the West were free of it. It was a group in Utah, not some Southeast Asian body, that used cash, credit cards, scholarships and gifts to persuade the International Olympic Committee (IOC) to choose their state as the site of the 2002 Winter Olympics. And, reading about the cronyism and waste which a special investigation into the European Commission uncovered in early 1999, what conclusions might Asians draw? The scandals in Salt Lake City and Brussels, coming so close together, are enough to persuade them that those who think only Asians are corrupt are either hypocritical or have not looked at themselves hard enough. With the more recent revelations of fraud and theft by powerful CEOs earning enormous salaries and perks thrown up by the collapse of Enron and Worldcom, as well as the role played by prestigious Wall Street investment banks and auditing firms in many of these crimes, people elsewhere might be excused for thinking that corporate America is utterly rotten.

An American example which Asians certainly shouldn't follow is the allocation of pork-barrel funds for projects designed to win votes for politicians. Pork-barrelling, a recurring source of corruption that leads to poor-quality investment in the West, is often no more than a division of the spoils among politicians. The politics of patronage, in all its forms, are reprehensible, Western pork-barrelling no less than Asian cronyism.

Besides, if cronyism in Asia were so terrible, why did American investors race European investors to sink money into Asian countries in the boom years, knowing a great chunk would go into corrupt families and business cliques? Foreign lenders and investors knew what they did. Or if they did not, then what did they have research departments for?

They rushed out quickly enough too. It was to shield the country from these rapid shifts of global money, and to buy time, that Mahathir imposed exchange controls on the Malaysian currency. The instant worldwide criticisms of these controls made it appear as though people understood these huge money flows and their impact on economies, when they might have more humbly confessed, as Krugman did, that they did not. "Now suppose that you were to buy a copy of the bestselling textbook on international economics," Krugman said, "What could it tell you about how to cope with such a sudden loss of confidence by international investors? Well, not much. Trust me—I'm the co-author of that textbook." A year later, a turn of the tide in the economy allowed Mahathir to claim vindication for his moves.

Mahathir's strategy for fixing the economy was a complete reversal of that of his finance minister and handpicked successor, Anwar Ibrahim. His subsequent dismissal followed by his arrest on criminal charges in rapid succession were inevitably linked by many to the clash between the two men and seen as politically motivated. The emotional uproar in a shaken Malaysia and expressions of disapproval by a handful of governments in the region drowned out Mahathir's protestations that Anwar's dismissal and subsequent events were unrelated to policy or personal differences. As Anwar's supporters took to the streets in Malaysia itself, and dozens of new Internet sites debated his case, the international media talked of a People Power movement in the making. Among other things, Anwar had wanted to pursue IMF-style policies and let inefficient companies go bust. But this was the last thing Mahathir wanted, the creation of a Malay business class has been so close to his heart.

The crisis was certainly dismaying, crushing hopes in one of the world's most promising economies. It required a hard look at the way things had been going, and prompted mutterings of "reform" and "time for change." Inevitably, many thought that a change for the better implied saying goodbye to the NEP. Some even seized the crisis as evidence to discredit the policy, equating it with the politics of patronage and the cronyism that supposedly brought about our downfall.

Too much concentration on economics, however, will blind us to another unquantifiable aspect of the NEP's success. What has often been overlooked is how far it has restored Malay self-confidence. Among progressives in the West, poverty is seen as self-perpetuating. The children of the poor and ill-educated start school at a disadvantage, and soon fall behind. Without decent education or confidence in themselves, they find it hard to get jobs. Robbed of the self-respect that comes from earning a livelihood, they find it hard to sustain responsibilities. And so it goes on, in a circle. A similar sense of defeat might have burdened the Malay if the NEP hadn't broken the cumulative vicious circle described by Myrdal.

Has it never occurred to those who condemn the NEP to consider Malay self-respect and manhood? How would they feel if they were the nominal masters of their country but were bit-part players in the national economy? How would they feel if, in spite of being the host people, they lagged far behind foreign immigrants in the educational and wealth tables? How could anyone expect the Malays to stand for it? If for no other reason, Malay pride would have demanded a redressal. There would surely come a point when they would have said at last: "That's it. Enough. That's all we can stand."

But they were modest in their expectations, and the degree of advancement achieved under the NEP probably came as a surprise to them as much as it did to those who looked down upon them. Today there is no missing the Malays in the top echelons of public, corporate, professional and intellectual life. By now any doubts about the ability of the Malays should surely have been thoroughly dispelled.

The 1990s saw the rise of the New Malay, or *Melayu Baru*, a foil to the old myth of the Lazy Malay. Rustam Sani, a senior fellow at the Institute of Strategic and International Studies (ISIS) Malaysia, sees the emergence of this new breed as being "indicative of a profound cultural transformation among the Malays that has been brewing for some time now and has started to erupt in the 1990s." He writes: "Whereas Malay political attitudes since the time of Independence in the late 1950s had been marked by a lack of confidence—by a need to be constantly reassured of political dominance through asserting cultural symbols of distinctly Malay identity—the Malays of the 1990s are politically and economically more confident."

Not to take heart at this would be perverse. Yet some Chinese feel they have little to be cheerful about. Why? Because they feel that in the process of gestating the New Malay, their own interests have been hurt, unfairly so, and because they are worried that, having got this far, the New Malay would want to go farther, perhaps disadvantaging them again.

Their feeling that they have suffered unfairness, that the Malays have relegated them to non-*Bumiputera* second-class citizenship, probably prevents them from giving credit where due. For credit is indeed due to the Malays: for their sound management of the country and the economy, and for their racial tolerance. Imperfect as it is, Malaysia's racial equilibrium is in stark contrast to the ethnic clashes that make up today's headlines, clashes reported from all over the world—the former Yugoslavia, the former Soviet Union, India, Sri Lanka, Ireland, Lebanon, Israel, Rwanda ... the list is endless. In few multicultural societies can one say, as one can in Malaysia: all is quiet on the racial front.

Their sense of grievance is not the only thing preventing the Chinese from giving credit where due. In finding fault with Malaysia, the Chinese (and Indians too) are also unwittingly influenced by Western rhetoric and dogma. Chauvinism and racial prejudice lurks in every nation. Yet the idea that Western democracies are somehow fairer and more tolerant dies hard. It persists in spite of evidence to the contrary. When immigrants are attacked in Germany, say, we blame the xenophobic Right of that country, as though far-Right violence was not German violence. When immigrants are attacked, even killed, in Britain, we blame the Skinheads and the National Front rather than British society.

Margaret Thatcher has said of the United States that "No other nation has so successfully combined people of different races and nations within a single culture." But tell that to the blacks in the squalid inner city slums and see if they agree. Yet it never occurs to anyone to question that remark and to wonder whether she has only the Germans, Jews, Irish and other white races in mind; to ask if she has factored non-whites into her equation. In many American cities whites are scared of straying into black housing projects and blacks feel nervous about driving through white streets. To appreciate the happier state of race relations in Malaysia, try substituting the words "whites" and "blacks" with "Malays" and "Chinese"—you will end up with a false statement. Yet we rarely draw such comparisons and remain unaware of the hold which the West's way of representing itself and others has on our perceptions.

We are in any event quicker to think well of the Westerners than we are of the Malays. For the Chinese, this comes of a habit of feeling superior to the Malays. I have sketched the historical background to this sense of superiority and shall not elaborate on it here, except to say that the tendency to respect white views is shared by the Indians in Malaysia and may be linked to the colonial mentality. The Chinese think that the West is siding with them when it calls for level playing fields, and that they must be right if the West is on their side. When other nations, such as Thailand, Korea and Indonesia, turned to the IMF, cap in hand, for help in calming panicked markets and Malaysia did not, the Chinese saw this as a case of Malaysia resisting the institutional changes—such as the removal of the NEP—that the IMF would demand as part of its rescue package.

They believed that IMF prescriptions would benefit the Chinese, a view hard to hold on to if one were to consider the disasters which befell the Chinese in Indonesia, where IMF pressure to adopt tough measures made life bleaker for the poor and riled up local politics. The Chinese seem to be unaware that many economists have put the blame on the IMF itself for the dismal condition of the Latin American economies—long the wards of the IMF. These days, there are suggestions that the IMF is not only incompetent but there may exist what is called the Wall Street-Treasury-IMF axis whose working, in the words of Professor Jagdish Bhagwati of Columbia University, "contribute little to the global economy but profit enormously by pretending that it does."

In the West, immigrants are sometimes told, in graffiti or in verbal abuses hurled at them, to "Go home." For us Malaysia-born Chinese, "home" is Penang or Kuala Lumpur or Ipoh. It is assuredly not China. But still it is a useful exercise to consider how we would have fared if our forbears had remained in Guangdong or Fujian. We would have been sent down to the countryside to toil alongside peasants during the Cultural Revolution, most likely, and we would be a lot poorer, most certainly—that is if we weren't among the 30 million people killed by the famine that followed in the wake of the Great Leap Forward. For those from the Indian subcontinent too, comparing their adopted home with their ancestral ones, whether India or Sri Lanka, will prove a chastening experience.

But I can see that the non-Malays will continue to begrudge Malaysia the credit which ought to be given it so long as they feel somehow they haven't been treated right by the Malays. Perception and attitudes will only change in the absence of any corroboration from actuality. Perception and attitudes survive when they have some direct relationship, however tenuous, to what is going on; otherwise they will wither, though usually after a time lag. In this case the corroboration is the differentiation made between *Bumiputeras* and non-*Bumiputeras*, and the perceived injury to the interests of the non-Malays inflicted by the NEP. The NEP is what sours communal relations. The division of society into fixed racial groups necessitated by the NEP nourishes their sense of apartness. The desirable effects of the NEP, then, are bought at a stiff price of racial polarisation, though it is probably true to say that if the NEP didn't exist and the Malays were pauperised or reduced, the racial polarisation would have been even worse.

The NEP favours a particular interest group in the name of the general interest, namely a better economic balance, which in turn makes for greater stability. The trouble is that the general interest in any society is much more often related to ends than to means. People who say that they are not against affirmative action as such, only against quotas, are disagreeing not with the ends but the means. Similarly, you can wholeheartedly endorse the idea of creating a Malay business class without being equally enthusiastic about the means adopted towards that end—the privatisation programme.

In *The Way Forward* (1998), Mahathir outlined his bid to create instant Malay tycoons at the same time as the country embarked on its privatisation of state-owned enterprises. Here was a chance, Mahathir thought, to create Malay-owned businesses of the size and ilk of the largest and most successful non-Malay conglomerates. The chance was seized and a number of franchises and companies were sold off to Malay entrepreneurs who were thereby helped to move directly into big business. Mahathir's reasoning is that unless Malay big business matched the scale and vigour of Chinese and foreign big business, the NEP would fail in its aims and race would continue to be identified with economic function. However, while he makes the case for the need for Malay big tycoons well enough, the case for how to set about fulfilling that need is less convincing. How are these individuals selected? Not through favouritism, Mahathir says, refuting the charge of cronyism. But Malays who failed to be picked remain sceptical, and who can blame them? Besides, it will take more than mere share ownership to make a successful entrepreneur.

But to give them to a small number of individuals is to raise questions about the propriety of such a policy and create an atmosphere where entrepreneurs instead of working on building businesses occupied themselves on finding quick windfalls. Meanwhile the decent majority ate their hearts out watching the spoils being taken by the few and restrained by good manners (or for fear of appearing jealous) kept silent.

As to the need for Malay tycoons, Li Ka-Shing is a role model of the rags-to-riches kind. The legendary Jack Welch of General Electric (GE) is a role model of the corporate kind. He is as worthy of emulation as Li Ka-Shing although he does not own a big chunk of his company. Jack Welch has probably more economic clout than Li Ka-Shing as he heads a much larger corporation. Malays already have many role models of the Jack Welch kind. Of the 10 largest Malaysian corporations in the Kuala Lumpur Stock Exchange (KLSE) in June 2003, eight have Malay CEOs. Petronas (not listed), the national oil company and a *Fortune* 500 company with a global operation, was first headed by Azizan Abidin and now Hassan Marican. All these CEOs have run large Malaysian corporations successfully for years. And in one important aspect they are a model for all, not just Malays because they don't demand outrageous compensations like some other CEOs. According to 2002 company records the pay of these CEOs ranges from US$95,000 to US$400,000 per annum (companies controlled by government at the lower end of the range), a far cry from the tens of millions contracted for American CEOs, many of whom ruined their investors and employees. For some reason these Malay CEOs have not been held up as role models and yet professional managers such as them are indispensable in the modern economy, more than the flashy tycoons.

Malays aspiring to be tycoons of the Li Ka-Shing kind must serve their time and risk their own money to pursue their ambition. Azman Hashim qualifies as one. Trained as an accountant he served his time in central and commercial banking and went on to risk his own money and build his AmBank Group singlehandedly. Two others were cited recently by Mahathir as role models. One is Syed Mokhtar Albukhary who started as a small rice miller in Kedah in partnership with Chinese some twenty years ago and today is successful and generous enough to build and donate the Islamic Arts Museum to the nation. The other is Mustapha Kamal. Starting as a minor bureaucrat he went on to work for a state-owned property development enterprise. He then went into the property business himself and has built up in less than 20 years a major property group.

Coming back to Mahathir's plan to create instant tycoons, many of those who had been propelled to the super-league by the programme, were badly hit by the Asian financial crisis and the majority of them wiped out. A comment by Daim Zainuddin, the former finance minister, explains why: "A lot of fellows get privatised projects and they have no experience. They're only interested in getting a project and pumping it into a listed company, see those shares fly. And then they borrow against the scrip. They want to get rich quickly and they forget about management. This must stop."

The way privatisation worked out, was certainly not without some flaws. Yet are the lapses reason enough to invalidate the whole NEP? Do we throw out the baby with the bath water? I don't think so, but I nevertheless doubt if there is a quick answer to the practical question of how authentic Malay capitalists are to emerge. This is the dilemma at the heart of the NEP: the difficulty of reconciling the ends with the means.

Besides, even given general agreement over ends, any policy which is adopted will hurt some people more than others, will benefit some groups at others' expense; and conflict will arise out of a situation in which, while a general interest is apparent in terms of ends, separate and divergent interests become apparent once means are put forward.

This too is the dilemma for the NEP: the difficulty of reconciling the general with the particular, of reconciling the interests of society as a whole with the interests of certain sections of society. Ask a Chinese whether he is in favour of a policy aimed at the betterment of chances for all groups in society and he will probably say yes. But ask him how that aim is to be achieved and he will probably say: through means that don't hurt me please. And when he is hurt, or hears of friends or relatives being hurt, then not only will he deplore the means but he will come to see the whole aim of the policy as working against him. The government pursues the aim in the name of the general interest, but he comes to see the general interest as merely a cloak for the special interests which it represents.

It is like governments declaring, "We all want peace," to say which is equivalent to saying, in the domestic context, that everyone wants prosperity and stability. But the agreement over ends is seldom accompanied by an agreement over means. Every country wants peace, but at its own price. For instance, a country may not accept a peace that entails its disarmament or its giving up disputed territory. Similarly, every country wants prosperity, but at its own price. What each interest wants is its own sort of peace or prosperity.

If it cannot get this it is usually prepared to accept rather different forms of peace or prosperity, so long as these are not positively detrimental to it. The Chinese may feel that they have had to accept a rather different form of prosperity since the institution of the NEP. But it is prosperity nonetheless. Individual interests have been hurt, yes, but many others, including the Chinese poor, have been relatively substantial gainers.

Elsewhere in the world, the demands of ethnically-based sectional interests are undermining national integration. The world is littered with the wrecks of governments which tried to combine diverse racial or linguistic or religious groups within a single state. This fact, coupled with the backlash against immigrants in the world's advanced countries, has given multiethnic societies a bad name. Yet I would argue that, far from seeing the diversity in Malaysia as a minus, we should see it as a plus.

History has given us a valuable racial mix. Combine this with the legacies of British rule and we have a country that is well placed to exploit the largest markets of the world, namely China, India, Southeast Asia and the English-speaking and Muslim worlds. It is fashionable nowadays to speak of business networks and relationships. Malaysians should cash in on the ready-made networks implied by its mix of peoples. What a hand of cards!

To have Malays and Chinese working at cross purposes would hardly be good for business. If the Malays feel themselves the masters of their own destinies, this is something the other races should rejoice in, because it is when we are afraid for ourselves that we hit out at others. Their aspirations raised by their success, they are setting their sights on becoming a model Islamic nation. They have something at stake, therefore, in a standard of national well-being measured not only by material yardsticks but by academic, cultural and spiritual ones. That this is so is also something the other races should rejoice in, because to prove people wrong when they perpetuate cultural stereotypes about Islamic backwardness, inequality and extremism is to work towards the antitheses of these qualities, and this can only mean higher standards of performance, behaviour and tolerance.

All this augurs well for the future. Yet we mustn't think that success is assured. In a world as fast-changing and as volatile as ours, nothing can be taken for granted and I am sure even bigger challenges await Malaysia. Will we have it in us to bring the right attitudes to bear on what lies ahead? This is a question I shall attempt to address in the next and final chapter.

CHAPTER 15

LOOKING AHEAD

IT IS A TRUISM that the future is unknowable. In heading this chapter "Looking Ahead," my intention is not to prophesy. All forecasts of the future are really extrapolations from the past and present. Yesterday and today shape the way in which tomorrow emerges.

So if I am optimistic about Malaysia's coming years, it is partly because it has a pretty good track record. The country has proved to be very resilient. In my view, Malaysia has undergone half a dozen great trials; it came through each without falling apart. The first test was Independence. Doubts were expressed about the viability of Malay statehood. A good number of British firms sold their businesses in Malaya ahead of a repeat of the African and Indian scenarios. But those with the faith and foresight to see bright prospects ahead were rewarded. Remember the late Lee Loy Seng, who bought up British estates cheaply and created the giant plantation group KL-Kepong Bhd?

The separation of Singapore from the Malaysian Federation in 1965 barely three years after its formation served as the next test. Continuous bickering and escalating tensions led to the momentous decision by the then Prime Minister, Tunku Abdul Rahman, to let Singapore secede and gain independence from the Federation. The extraordinary nature of this decision cannot be overemphasised—nations have been known to go to war over a sliver of uninhabited territory and yet the leadership was willing to give up a whole prosperous island without firing a shot. The leadership held firm against protests and, as it turned out, the decision benefited both Singapore and Malaysia. Had separation not occurred, the way things were going, the country would surely have been distracted by tensions and conflicts to the detriment of its development, if not worse. In this, the Malay leadership had demonstrated magnanimity and willingness to make courageous and far-sighted decisions for the well-being of all its people.

These same leadership qualities were again evident in the way they handled the Communist insurgency. Having been effectively contained, the MCP became a spent force, reduced to little more than a few bands of increasingly disillusioned armed partisans operating in jungle areas along the Malaysia-Thai border. In time it would have dwindled to a complete and inglorious end, and yet the government with the cooperation of the pragmatic Thais, accorded Chin Peng, the communist leader, "face" by signing the Haadyai Peace Accord with him in 1989, thus bringing to a formal and early end the MCP's armed struggle and the return to society, with a measure of dignity, of the 1,200 remnants of their futile struggle. Had the government insisted on the conventional legalistic approach, the problem would have festered to the detriment of the country's peace and progress.

Not long after the separation of Singapore from Malaysia came the race riots of May 1969. Parliament was suspended following the unrest and in a move that many foresaw as a step towards autocracy, the National Operations Council (NOC) took control of the running of the country. "I told you so," said those who had sold their interests at *Merdeka*. Yet, to the surprise of sceptics and against the expectations of those who offloaded their assets or left the country, Parliament was restored within two years, and Malaysia held together and grew.

Then came the great recession of the mid-1980s. The over-confidence of the government and the excesses of the corporate sector combined to make this a downturn the likes of which Malaysia had never seen before. Its consequences left no one unscathed, whether tycoon or shopkeeper, professional or clerk. Thousands of small people, mostly Chinese, went abroad without any help to work illegally in Taiwan, Japan, Australia, the United States and elsewhere and remitted hundreds of millions of ringgit back to support their families in Malaysia.

Many of the big corporate names were wiped out. One of the casualties was Multi-Purpose Holdings, the investment arm of the MCA and the Chinese answer to the *Bumiputera* corporate onslaught. It went into receivership and was ignominiously sold for a pittance. Those who had quit the country now felt vindicated in their decision, and barely disguised their perverse satisfaction in pointing out that Malaysia had come unstuck. The Malays had messed it up.

Lee Shin Cheng seized the opportunity to expand and created another giant plantation and property group, IOI. His good fortune is shared by those who managed to hang on during the recession—by using both legal delaying tactics and other more unconventional means—to emerge with fattened wallets. Malaysia not only pressed on but forged ahead, chalking up one year of spectacular growth after another.

But good times never roll on forever and, come the second half of 1997, economic turmoil engulfed Malaysia as swiftly as it engulfed other Asian and emerging markets. This was the next great test. Severely tested by the crisis, Malaysia has yet managed to remain stable. Far from shattering like Indonesia, Malaysia stayed whole. No Malay whipped himself into frenzies of anti-Chinese feeling. No Malay mob scapegoated the Chinese. Surely it is easy to see that, were it not for the NEP, poor aggrieved Malays would be striking for justice—against those whom they perceive as rich Chinese?

All this is reason for us to be confident about our country. Post-*Merdeka* track record apart, my other reason for a rosy view is the character of our people. I often wonder what would have happened if our racial composition had been different. I cannot help but feel that the outcome would have been less favourable. Against the pressures threatening to set Malays and Chinese apart is the countervailing force of tolerance. What the Malays have most conspicuously shown has been an attitude of accommodation. In a series of articles published in the *New Straits Times*, Chandra Muzaffar, then the Senior Research Fellow at the Centre for Policy Research at Universiti Sains Malaysia (USM), explains that this acceptance is embedded in Islamic culture and reflects "a larger world view which has found expression at different times and in different climes right through Muslim history." The Chinese, for their part, are a forbearing people and probably the most governable on earth. They do not easily resort to violence and will, in their characteristically long-suffering fashion, put up with a great deal for the sake of peace.

I take heart from other Malay characteristics: their organisational and administrative skills, their political savvy. The UMNO party machinery is probably one of the world's most formidable. In the business and professional fields, the management skills they show are all the more remarkable for the rapidity with which they have been acquired. What's more, they are high spenders—which is certainly good news to the Chinese shopkeeper!

As for the Chinese, there are few people to match them for industriousness. Besides, they like to keep their heads down and mind their own business. They are economically self-sustaining, not at all the kind to depend on others or demand handouts, so they can never be liabilities. Even the humblest of them try their best to make it on their own and stand on their own feet. They are quick to seize every little opportunity to which others would not give a second look. They are quietly but fiercely competitive in the manner they know best—by offering cheaper prices—which is good news to the Malay consumer. They are not afraid of risks when it comes to investing their money. And they are probably the world's most sporting losers: they will almost always blame themselves for their losses, putting them down to their own greed or stupidity rather than to a rigged race or market. It is for these reasons that the Chinese have become in the words of Mahathir "necessary even to the Malays" and you can also say: to the Thais, the Filipinos, the Indonesians and so on.

They contribute to the country's prosperity in big ways and small. Earlier I mentioned that when Malaysia experienced its deep recession in the mid-1980s, some 70,000 Chinese went abroad to work and repatriated their earnings, thereby injecting multi-billions into the economy. Similarly, a great deal of what the Chinese earn can be recouped by the government. How? Through the famed Chinese penchant for gambling, of course. Stamp duty on stock market share transactions, and gaming taxes from racing, casinos and lotteries swell the government coffers. Add to all this the amount gained through excise and import duties on alcoholic drinks and it will be seen that the Chinese contribute many billions a year to government revenue.

Just as I believe we would have done less well were we a different mix of peoples, so I think we were lucky to have had the British for our colonialist. We might have had the Dutch or the Portuguese; after all, they ruled Malacca before the British came along. The British were better tutors on the tools for modern economic management: a supporting framework of laws and institutions, a working administrative system. Look around Southeast Asia and see if you don't agree. It wasn't a matter of just take, take, take. Indeed those pioneers ran the colony at a very moderate cost. The big gains were enjoyed by the investors of the City of London, but even there the profits were fairly modest—as was demonstrated by the ease with which Malaysian private companies and government agencies bought back the British mining companies, plantations and trading houses upon Independence. As for the managers and administrators in the field, they were far from living in clover. Many of them now live out their retirement on modest pensions.

If my optimism is grounded in the country's track record and its human capital, it is also encouraged by Malaysia's aspirations and by the international trends impinging on our evolution. In the previous chapter I explained why we should draw comfort from the Malays' wish to present their country as a showcase of Islam. Better to have a government that sets itself ever higher standards, I reckon, than one which just muddles along. Malaysia wishes to champion the Third World, to display a commitment to South-South trade and to play a key part on the regional and international stages. Its self-appointed role as a spokesman for the non-aligned group of nations and the high profile it adopts in the East Asian Economic Caucus (EAEC) are reflections of its ambitions in the international arena. The Malays want international "face," and to gain "face" you must be seen to be progressive and successful.

They will also continue to need foreign investment. The globalisation of capital is now a given. The rules governing the flow of money are pretty much the same worldwide: the eyes of the world—in the form of the IMF, the WTO, the World Bank, the Asian Development Bank (ADB), rating agencies like Standard & Poor's (S&P's) and Moody's Investor Service, and international fund managers—will be upon Malaysia as never before. And just as Indonesia, for example, displayed a new tolerance towards its industrial workers because the Clinton administration in the U.S. had said that the U.S.'s renewal of Indonesia's trade privileges under the generalised system of preferences hinged on its treatment of organised labour, so Malaysia faces a range of international pressures to liberalise, and to be evenhanded in its handling of race matters.

Malaysia is increasingly hooked up to the global marketplace. The broader economic and social trends—privatisation, freer trade, democratisation, human rights, consumerism, environmentalism—will help integrate the races in ways large and small. With market forces governing the management of post-national corporations like Telecom Malaysia, and with the marketplace for goods and labour becoming more open and competitive, citizens and consumers will increasingly be able—through their participation or preferences—to bend policies and decisions in a more accountable and non-discriminatory direction. Just the need to deliver profits means that your decisions will have less to do with politics—and, by extension, race—than economics. Even the hawker you used to pass on your way to work is moving his pitch from the street into the coffeeshop—a change signifying a deregulation of sorts, however lowly.

With privatisation, education too becomes less contentious. New private colleges with degree programmes twinned with those of Western universities are sprouting up by the dozen, offering menus of courses not available in Malaysia before. In addition, the Merdeka University mentioned earlier, long the dream of the Chinese community, has just come into being as the Universiti Tunku Abdul Rahman (UTAR). The Indians too now have their Asia Institute of Medical Sciences and Technology (AIMST). And the government now talks of creating an education industry catering to not just Malaysia but the region. Education has in fact become just another consumer product. The roadblocks on the path to higher education have been easing for some years already—and with them, one of the main sources of Chinese discontent.

For many non-Malays in the early stages of NEP, to be denied a job in government was to be left without a lifeline. This is hardly the case now, with jobs being so plentiful—and so much better paid—in the private sector. Of course, those who harbour political ambitions or those attracted to public service may feel some frustration. In traditional Chinese society, you were only deemed to have arrived when you became an official. But since when have middlemen minorities been welcomed into any bureaucracy?

To come back to Malaysia's aspirations, Mahathir has urged the country to rally around the goal he calls Vision 2020, which aims to make Malaysia a fully developed industrial nation within one generation. To go by the catchphrases that one hears, this is not just a matter of upgrading ourselves economically but also "morally" and "ethically."

Is this no more than a political slogan? I think not, if only because Mahathir has always been dead serious in his undertakings. What it indicates is that the government is framing still more ambitious national agendas and looking to meet still greater challenges ahead. Indeed the Malays are frequently told by their leaders to improve their performance in this or that sphere. As a community they appear to be constantly lifting their game.

Where will the Chinese be in all these changes? First, the bad news: our numbers are falling, and the projections are that by the year 2070, we may make up only 13 per cent of the total national population, a considerable drop from the 31 per cent we constitute at present. Our lower birth rate compared to that of the Malays is of course linked to our high rate of urban migration. The dwindling proportion makes the Chinese fret, but it need not. We don't know how urbanised the Malays will be in 2070, two and a half generations from now, and it may be that as they urbanise and their birth rate falls—and birth rates invariably fall with urbanisation—their population growth relative to that of the Chinese may turn out to be smaller than has been projected. Nevertheless, the Chinese are worried that the Malays will crowd them out.

Optimists say that Malay urbanisation will, by broadening the areas of interaction, help to integrate the races; pessimists say that it will intensify the rat race and spur competition and conflict. Whichever of these projections proves true, one scenario that will not arise is the old one of Malays and Chinese meeting only as peasant customers and creditor shopkeepers.

The Chinese can look at increasing Malay numbers in one of two ways: as a threat or as an enlarged market. One view they would be foolish to take would be that they could dominate. If they're in any doubt about this, just take a headcount. Their situation is analogous to that of the West, whose population of 800 million people pales beside the almost 4.7 billion made up by the rest of the world. Kishore Mahbubani notes in an essay he published in 1993 that, "In the national arena, no Western society would accept a situation where 15 per cent of its population legislated for the remaining 85 per cent. But this is what the West is trying to do globally." The author calls it a folly. Mahbubani is a diplomat from Singapore, a predominantly Chinese society which would do well to remember, every time it is tempted to swagger, that its numbers are puny compared to the non-Chinese countries by whom it is surrounded.

Whatever happens, the ascendancy of the Malays in all areas of Malaysian life will not be in any doubt. In the colonial breakdown of business, British and other European interests were paramount in finance and infrastructure; now such interests are predominantly Malay. One advantage the Malays have and the Chinese do not is their control of institutional funds like the EPF, PNB, LTAT and Tabung Haji, which ensure control of major Malaysian corporations like Maybank, Sime Darby and MISC. In addition, the government still directly controls Petronas, Tenaga Nasional Bhd (TNB) and Telekom. These companies pack a big financial punch.

Where does that leave us Chinese? In the economic field, I see us playing the role we are best at and most enjoy: that of the middleman. There are those of us who have the organisational muscle to run big enterprises, but most of us will continue to thrive in the small and medium-sized enterprises (SMEs), a sector conducive to wealth creation (as has been demonstrated by Taiwan, a nation of SMEs).

Plainly there is a place for us, and by no means an insignificant one at that. As our prosperity shows, we have been left plenty of room to flex our muscles. It is true that nobody has declared an end to state intervention; that still exists in the form of the NDP. But when I add in all the trends I see around me, I am left with the conclusion that the future will offer the Chinese still greater opportunities. Indeed, many have observed that the *average* Chinese in Malaysia today has more economic opportunities than his counterparts in Singapore, Thailand, Indonesia, Philippines or in Hong Kong or Taiwan and paradoxically thanks to the NEP. In any event, the immigrant Chinese would hardly be prime candidates for heroship in the literature on Southeast Asia if they hadn't shown themselves to be a match for their challengers. Take away the gauntlet of economic competition, and we will become plump and complacent.

More importantly, I believe the Malays are too astute not to realise that free lunches cannot go on forever. Free lunches are an expensive habit, and not even two of the world's richest countries, Kuwait and Brunei, can sustain it. Much of the cost of the free lunches was in fact paid out of the country's accumulated reserves, and reserves are finite.

The huge capital requirements of a country aspiring to developed-country status by 2020 will mean that Malaysia would have to create much more wealth to pay for infrastructure and other needs. For this undertaking, the Malays are now self-confident enough, I believe, to enlist the entrepreneurial drive and capital of the Chinese. The alternative is drafting in more foreigners—the devils you don't know!

So far I've been discussing prospects for the Chinese community with reference to the country as a whole and to where the Malays are headed. That still leaves the Chinese dilemma. Do I have any reasons for thinking that we will—or at least should—become less disgruntled, distrustful and defensive? The financial crisis raised the spectre of division, between the intelligentsia who believe Anwar could deliver modernity, including Western-style democracy; and those (Chinese businessmen among them) who look to Mahathir for stability and who, in their fear of the resurgence of Islamic fundamentalism, ask if Malaysia would now go backwards. Although the Chinese were mere bystanders in the conflict between Mahathir and Anwar, still they were faced with a choice: to go with what Anwar represented, or with what Mahathir stood for? How are they to play their cards?

If I may recapitulate: many individual Chinese were hurt by the NEP and they are still saying "Ouch." That is one issue. Another is the question, "Is this a short sharp shock or is there more in store?" A third is political peripheralisation. Fourth is loss of cultural identity.

To take these issues one at a time: I know it's hard to put the past behind us, and I perfectly understand the pain and disaffection of those who cry "Ouch." Yet we Chinese have always been good at saying, "*Suan le*" ("Forget it," or "Let it be") and getting on with the next task. Happily, one thing we are not known for doing is scratching bitterly at our sores. It may help us to shake off the hangovers from the past if we remind ourselves that things had to get much worse before they became better.

I realise that forgetting is the easy part; the hard part is to feel reassured that there would be no more to pay. The renewal of the NEP as the NDP encourages many Chinese in their suspicion that Malays want bigger helpings. But I would argue against undue Chinese anxiety by pointing to the rise of the New Malay and to the Malay moves to lift their game. No one who wants to walk tall would want to walk with crutches. The Malay leadership is certainly not insensitive to the dangers of perpetuating a culture of dependence and Mahathir has increasingly and somewhat exasperatingly, called on Malays to do away with crutches.

Of course Malay religious fanaticism is the wild card in the pack. What can we do to minimise our uneasiness? Here a consideration of the mainstream's interests can offer guidance. Religious extremism is no less a headache to the government (with its wish for Malaysia to be a progressive Muslim showcase) than it is to the Chinese. A sense of mutual interest should join us Chinese with the Malay mainstream. For our own sake as well as the country's, we need to inject ourselves into alliances with the Malay moderates. Now perhaps more than at any other time there is a need for the Chinese to demonstrate their commitment to the partnership with Malays. In this regard there have been a number of occasions in the past where the Chinese appeared to have tried to extract concession from the Malay leadership just at the time when they were facing critical divisions within UMNO or the Malay community. The Chinese should now realise that their well-being is not threatened by the strength and prosperity of the Malays. The threat will come from the disunity and impoverishment of the Malays.

What we must not be persuaded to do is to play "chicken," the game where two cars drive head-on towards each other and then, just as they are about to hit each other, veer off. It is a game which positively invites accidents. The riots of May 1969 was one such accident and the Chinese education crisis in 1987 or the Suqiu in 2000 could have been another. So we must not allow ourselves to be tempted or goaded into pitting ourselves recklessly against the Malays—for that way lies violence. Chinese defiance will provoke Malay reaction, and it cannot be assumed that violence will be absent in any future conflict. Come another May 1969 crisis, and there will be far worse to follow. Violence breeds violence; once it is resorted to, it ceases to be of any use as a deterrent.

What about political peripheralisation? The Chinese feel that, while their interests cannot be entirely gainsaid in Malaysia, they have no hope of achieving power. At best they can defend their communal position, not improve it. At the back of their minds is the feeling that, "It is their country, their show. The only roles left to us to play are supporting or subordinate ones."

This translates into a less than wholehearted identification with Malaysia, so that any rallying call by the government is bound to fire them with less enthusiasm than the Malays. The Malays are propelled forward by their pride in their country and their desire to enhance its world standing, but the Chinese, sharing little of this nationalism or ambition, are inclined to hang back. The magnitude of Malay and Chinese aims is different: national in the one, merely communal in the other. Searching for a platform capable of appealing to the majority of Chinese voters, our politicians can only come up with the defence of Chinese rights, chiefly the right to primary school education in the Chinese medium.

Yet the future of Malaysia is held in collective hands, not just Malay ones. It does neither us nor the country much good to be narrowly concerned with communal self-interests. Why limit our horizons when the Malays are widening theirs? Why discount the possibility of a Chinese, or part-Chinese, becoming prime minister one day? It has happened in Thailand and the Philippines. We shall only ever have political lightweights for leaders if all we ever fight is rearguard action. We would do well, I think, to set a broader agenda and evolve a larger sense of purpose.

Easier said than done, some readers will say. It takes two to tango, and you can't be part of something that doesn't want you. As Malaysia strives towards Vision 2020, the Malays will have wholehearted and patriotic Chinese on board only if the Chinese feel that it is every bit their future as well. In this connection it will make a difference to their degree of commitment whether or not they feel they have an equal stake in the nation's future and in its world standing. The Malays need to reach out to the Chinese, and accord them the respect they require and deserve.

Finally, the issue of Chinese identity and its companion, Chinese-language education. Once upon a time, to be Chinese was to be loyal to China. The Chinese in Malaysia and the rest of Southeast Asia were viewed with suspicion by their host governments as people who owed their first allegiance to China. Family ties to the homeland were stronger then, and China keener to win the hearts and minds of its emigrants.

Nowadays, loyalty simply doesn't come into it. Ties are tenuous, if they exist at all, and, truth to tell, Malaysian Chinese of the younger generation are not much more at home in China than they are in Vietnam, say, or Indonesia. Today they look at it as a market like any other, or a place where they could do business and, if they are lucky, make money. If their Chinese origin helps smooth their path, that is all to the good; they would not be successful businessmen if they didn't exploit every advantage. The opening of China allowed overseas Chinese to see China for what it is: a backward country where corruption is rife, despite the spectacular economic development achieved over the past two decades.

What is at issue today is not divided loyalties (to China on the one hand, and Malaysia on the other) but minority rights. Malay is the national language and identity, agreed. But the extent of cultural and linguistic diversity below the level of the nation remains controversial. I don't, however, expect it to remain contentious in the long term, because I see more and more young Chinese disappearing into the ranks of the Malay- and English-educated. In the long run, to use literacy in Mandarin as a means of maintaining Chinese culture outside China will prove too difficult in the absence of fresh immigration. If even Singapore, with a Chinese majority, is finding it uphill work, how much harder will it be for Malaysia.

Before I end I should try to trace the source of my own acceptance of affirmative action in Malaysia. I suspect my empathy has its origin in my childhood when as a small boy before the war I often listened to stories told by my mother about Japanese atrocities in China such as the Nanjing Massacre and tales of Chinese humiliation at the hands of Western imperial powers—there were supposedly signs at the entrance to public parks in the foreign concessions in Shanghai which read "Dogs and Chinese not allowed." Even at that tender age I could feel surges of anger at the Japanese and white man made worse by a feeling of helplessness. Also as a young man I worked in the rural areas with Malays attending to projects in padi fields, and in remote areas where only Malays lived. It was obvious they were living in poverty and somehow they always seemed to carry themselves with simple dignity. I used to wonder what would happen to me if I was raised in a Malay peasant family. As mentioned earlier in the story I later became involved in business where I met Chinese businessmen who were completely oblivious of *The Malay Dilemma* and whose sole concern was the Chinese predicament. Therefore when I first read *The Malay Dilemma* it was easy for me to identify with the poverty and humiliation of the Malays and the explosive feelings mentioned by Mahathir. I have always thought that if there was a race that could understand *The Malay Dilemma* it would have been us Chinese.

I will end with a quote from a young black American who wrote a book called *Native Stranger* on his travels in Africa. He finds that he hates it there: the filth, the corruption, the greed. Looking for a lesson from Africa for the blacks back home, he finds it, by a strange irony, not in black Africa but in white South Africa, not in a black African but in a white Boer (Dutch-descended South African). Neither a black American nor a white South African, he says, has anywhere else to go now: "He is here to stay, so he will have to make it work or lose it all here."

Make it work or lose it all here. Here is a lesson for us Chinese Malaysians to bear in mind too.

SUGGESTED READING

Gurr, Ted Robert, *Minorities at Risk: A Global View of Ethnopolitical Conflicts* (Washington, D.C.: United States Institute of Peace Press, 1993)

Harris, Eddy L., *Native Stranger: A Black American's Journey into the Heart of Africa* (New York: Simon & Schuster, 1992)

Mahathir Mohamad, *A New Deal for Asia* (Subang Jaya: Pelanduk Publications, 1999)

Mahathir Mohamad, *The Challenge* (Petaling Jaya: Pelanduk Publications, 1986)

Mahathir Mohamad, *The Malay Dilemma* (Singapore: The Asia-Pacific Press, 1970)

Mahathir Mohamad, *The Way Forward* (London: Weidenfeld & Nicolson, 1998)

Myrdal, Gunnar, *An American Dilemma: The Negro Problem and Modern Democracy* (New York: Harper & Row, 1944)

Pan, Lynn, *Sons of the Yellow Emperor: The Story of the Overseas Chinese* (London: Mandarin, 1990)

Rehman Rashid, *A Malaysian Journey* (Kuala Lumpur: Rehman Rashid, 1993)

Sowell, Thomas, *Preferential Policies: An International Perspective* (New York: William Morrow, 1990)

INDEX

YE LIN-SHENG is a Malaysian businessman born to Chinese migrant parents who came to Malaya in 1931. He has run companies in Malaysia, Hong Kong and Australia, and has been involved in businesses in Thailand, China, Singapore, the United Kingdom and the United States. Ye was educated in Christian missionary schools and later studied engineering. He spent the early part of his career in government service during the colonial period working alongside Malays, Chinese and Indians. These beginnings and his subsequent experiences overseas have touched his reflections on the Chinese condition in Malaysia over 50 years. *The Chinese Dilemma* is the fruit of those reflections.